Keeping Heart on Pine Ridge

Vic Glover

Keeping Heart on Pine Ridge

family ties, warrior culture
commodity foods, rez dogs
and the Sacred

Vic Glover

Native Voices

Summertown, Tennessee

Cover photographs by Victor Glover
Cover design by Warren Jefferson
Book design by Jerry Lee Hutchens

Native Voices
Book Publishing Company
P.O. Box 99
Summertown, TN 38483
1-888-260-8458
www.bookpubco.com

07 06 05 04   4 3 2 1

ISBN 1-57067-165-6

Library of Congress Cataloging-in-Publication Data

Glover, Victor.
Keeping heart on Pine Ridge : family ties, warrior culture, commodity foods, rez
dogs, and the sacred / Victor Glover.
    p. cm.
ISBN 1-57067-165-6
1. Oglala Indians--South Dakota--Pine Ridge Indian Reservation--History. 2.
Oglala Indians--South Dakota--Pine Ridge Indian Reservation--Social life and
customs. 3. Pine Ridge Indian Reservation (S.D.)--History. 4. Pine Ridge Indian
Reservation (S.D.)--Social life and customs. I. Title.
E99.O3G56 2004
978.3004'9752--dc22
                              2004015878

This book is dedicated to the Oglala Lakota.

A heartfelt thanks is extended to all those

who encouraged the essays.

A further thanks is given to all those who

contributed to the publication of the book.

Contents

Generosity

First time I've ever had an Indian landlord. The rent's right-on, eighty-five bucks a month for this 15 x 30-foot log cabin rented from my Sun Dance brother, Fontanelle (Poncho) Afraid Of Bear. Before that, in the tipi down over the hill, the rent was free. This here is a paradisiacal writer's retreat disguised as a tar-paper drinker's shack, where you can't see a fence, the horizon extends for a hundred miles, the nighttime sky reveals a 180-degree panorama, and when you sit in the outhouse, you're gazing directly at Maki Zita, an ancient volcano and most prominent land feature, sitting a mile to the east.

You could say that many of us living up here have given up on the American dream, because we find that the values extolled and pursued by commercial, consumer-driven American society, in and of themselves are illusory, mythological, essentially empty, and selfishly unfulfilling. Where in American culture is the heart?

The outer culture seems selfish because most of Indian America isn't participating fully in the American dream. Maybe some Indians are prosperous, but most of the relatives around here are pretty pitiful. All of us are pitiful. We're always asking the Creator to take pity on us all.

People out there in the American world don't know how pitiful America's First Citizens really are. It's amazing how many of the alert, intelligent, open-minded, forward-thinking, well-intentioned, fortunate sons and daughters just two states away have no idea we're here. Despite us thinking we're the center of the universe, many people don't know where Pine Ridge Indian Reservation is, or that Wounded Knee happened here, or that Crazy Horse and Sitting Bull were Lakota.

They don't know that 67 percent of the population here lives in third-world poverty, and half the people over forty-five suffer from diabetes. People don't seem to know or care that there is more than 85 percent unemployment and an incredible rate of alcoholism and dysfunction, infant mortality, and teenage suicide. The enormity of the problems are as staggering as America's neglect. Like a stake in the heart.

My brother Tom likes to say, "We're surrounded by insurmountable opportunity."

And it's true. There are, in the midst of all this misery and daily suffering that leaves no family or individual untouched, enormous opportunities. Tom likes to create positive change, like building and renovating homes across the reservation, but most of the time, under the prevailing overwhelming circumstances, he's just treading water.

— — — — —

There are four cardinal virtues among the Lakota: Honesty. Courage. Humility. Generosity. A chief should possess and have refined them all. Some of the people have cultivated and mastered these elements of character, like the Old Man and Uncle Joe, the walking epitome of humility. Humility defeats pride. It dissipates defense mechanisms. It teaches us silence.

Just what is true humility? In the Old Man, it's like the wind.

Nothing sticks. But he does have an ego. We saw it a couple of weeks ago as he sat here drinking coffee one morning. He was remarking about the young, "overnight medicine men," saying, "That guy (referring to himself) over there . . . he knows a little something . . . but that guy over there (in the neighboring Sicangu band on Rosebud Reservation) . . . he knows IT ALL."

He said it again, and really got us laughing. Then he said it again. A good story or good joke never gets old around here. It's told repeatedly, usually teasingly, often distorted and stretched, in the presence of the person at whom it's aimed. You're not supposed to get uptight or take offense. You listen and laugh right along with everyone else. If you try to explain that that's not the way it went, or if you get upset, you . . . just . . . don't . . . get it.

— — — — —

And so, this old man, Ernest, is the spiritual leader of the Afraid Of Bear tiospaye (extended family). The oldest of seven brothers, he'd been a ceremonial fireman all his life for his younger brother, Larue, who conducted ceremony up until his death and was the family spiritual leader, premiere medicine man, peyote "road man" (leader), and whose vision we're currently carrying out at the Sun Dance in the Black Hills.

After hanging around those guys long enough, they eventually taught their songs . . . the first time in their lives they ever allowed their songs to be recorded, Loretta said. Songs passed down from their granddad, and his grandfather before him, Larue said, a lineage including the famed pre-reservation shaman, George Sword, who contributed the bulk of the knowledge contained in *Lakota Belief and Ritual*. The songs are cherished and held close to the heart. Prayer songs. Ceremonial songs. Just a small piece of the cultural richness.

Fragments carried over from an earlier time. They say the old people knew many things that have been lost, and we've only got a small piece of what once was. And here, too, is only a fragment of that small piece.

— — — — —

One could maybe get close to finding the heart of America in Native America. Indian people are the most giving people you'll find. Indian people have given everything to America, but they hold the heart. Within that heart lies the ceremonial life, spirit, and ways of the people, and within "The Ways" lies the essential nature of helping others.

At the center of The Ways is the Sun Dance, an annual celebration of life. They say we dance for The People. We go without food or water and give flesh and blood for The People. That offering is a sacrifice for The People. The Creator is looking down on this magnificent tree and ceremony in honor of all that is, and the pitiful people inside and outside the arbor . . . and the prayers sent toward the heavens are going to be heard.

Of course we're in there for ourselves. By helping others, we help ourselves. Sure. Although not a primary motive, many blessings flow from the sacrifice. We're going to clean ourselves out, for one.

Limits are discovered. One realizes that water and everything living are truly sacred. Courage may be found. One may learn something of humility, or honesty, or generosity. Maybe there could be a vision out there. Maybe we'll see.

My sister considers us pagans and says Jesus did all that suffering for us . . . we don't have to symbolically do what He did. It's taken care of, she says. We don't have to do all that, she says. But these folks were doing this Dance long before they were ever introduced to Jesus, and I asked Him, and Jesus told me it was okay. In fact, it brought tears to His eyes.

So yeah. In addition to The People, we're in there for ourselves . . . and our families. And then we realize just how big our family really is. And then after the Dance is over, one's load may get heavier. You've got 361 days to keep on dancing through life. Our daily walk is our dance.

"If you have . . . if your cup is full, you're expected to give," somebody said. The Creator sends people in need to us, and we can't say no. We're supposed to give, and give, and give, and keep on giving. Do that, and there's no need to worry about needs, Dad said. You belong to the Creator. He's gonna take care of you. And in the end, I guess we didn't need the Dance, or Jesus, to tell us that.

That's why that buffalo skull is on the altar. Like Jesus, the Creator sent that buffalo to the people to take care of their needs. And like Jesus, that buffalo, in a giveaway, laid down its life . . . gave its flesh and blood so The People could live. That's why it's considered sacred.

That's why it's on the altar.

General Phil Sheridan knew that. You kill all the buffalo, and you defeat The People. But then, General Sheridan didn't get them all.

Going for Wood

Probably shouldn't have tried just running on through that mucky area that turned out to be a drainage ditch. Went ahead anyway, because I was hot, tired, had sweat in my eyes, and my glasses were obscured by sweat and sawdust.

Just tossed the Stihl chainsaw in the back atop the wood, hopped in, and took what appeared to be the easiest way out of the ravine with a cord of wood piled up in the red, two-ton dump truck, "La Roja Grande" ("Big Red"). Felt good. Nice load. Headed out.

Not fast enough. Not fast enough to charge across that drainage ditch that was flowing from the windmill and cow-watering trough, about twenty feet away, which I should have had the sense to realize, but didn't.

Like I said, I had sweat in my eyes. It was hot. I was thirsty. "No damned excuse, man," I said to myself as I tried to extricate the truck from the muck.

"Nothin' stops La Roja," I said out loud to the air, since I was working alone and Lupe, my Mexican assistant, still hadn't yet returned from visiting his takojas (grandchildren) in Scottsbluff. She went, er, spun forward an inch, then back an inch, then forward, then back—slowly sinking down with the full load. About a cord, I'd say. Good load. Not quite up to the axles. The muck, not the load. The load was cab-high, up over the sideboards. Ash wood. Hot fire.

Got out, examined the wheels mired in muck, and tried bark and sticks under the dualie rear tires. Ha. Fat chance. Slim chance. Same thing. No way. First clue should've been the cattails and green-ass marsh grass, when everything else for five hundred miles is sun-fried brown this time of year. Shoulda known. Should've gone out the same way I came in.

The way I came in was on solid ground. "I'll be right back," I thought. "Better leave the saw in La Roja." Left the saw in La Roja and headed out on foot, across country. 'Bout a five mile walk, it turned out to be. That's the third time I've walked back from that spot, the mother lode of ash that we've been picking at for two years now.

Third time. First time, what happened? The starter went out on "Dorf," a squirrely, gray-primered half-ton, banged-up, piece-of-shit pickup truck. Second time, I got Dorf stuck in the snow. This time—no excuse. I wanted to lean against the hood of the truck and ask the first person to come along, "Could you kick me squarely in the ass, please?" but that would've been a long wait. Took my cigs and headed off to the east.

Off to the east, Maki Zita, the dormant volcano that they say the old folks can remember going off, looked closer than it really was, from the folds in the land. It looked the same size as it does from my back door, which I knew was five miles closer. That's just the way it appears . . . illusory, you could say . . . just like the land.

The land lies out here full of washes, draws, and ravines that you can't see until you get right up on top of them. Same thing happened to Custer up north when he and his men galloped up on top of the ridge and suddenly saw ALL THOSE INDIANS. Oops.

So that makes the walk further, don't it? Figuring you gotta go down into those ravines, and back up the other side, popping back up on top where you can see you're not much closer than you were on the other side. Illusory.

They'd have to come get me out. We were having a sweat lodge that night with the people from Colorado who wanted the Indians to plant garlic and wanted to take in a sweat. We were having a sweat, and I had all the wood. Besides that, since I'm the fireman, they'd have to pull me out.

Turned out, just as I got to the highway, Ernest, (commonly referred to by "the boys" as "the Old Man") came down the road and gave me a ride the last two miles. Junior, Ernest's teenage grandson, hopped back in the jump seat and let me have the front. When I told the Old Man that I'd buried La Roja with a full load of wood, he just said, "Wellllllllllll."

They were headed to town, but first they took me over to Beatrice's old place just over the hill where about a half dozen folks were meeting with the people from Colorado who wanted the Indians to plant garlic. Tom, his wife Loretta, her mom Beatrice, neighbor Sandy, Duane and Clayton from Porcupine, those three guys from Colorado, and Ernest, Junior, and me. They had soup, coffee, fry bread, red Kool-Aid and plum wojapi.

"That's a bit of a stretch," I thought, listening to their plan to curb teenage suicide on Pine Ridge by planting garlic—but the connections were there, along with the logic, in Archie's mind. Supplement the family income by planting garlic along with the vegetable gardens we already had going, and give The People some hope. You could almost see the connection. It was do-able, or at least worth a try.

Start an educational campaign, and get these kids out there, and . . . . Yeah. Suicide rate's gonna drop, right? Well . . . I don't know. I told 'em so. Maybe you could have an impact on a few tiospayes, or families, and then maybe it could expand from there, once the relatives see you turned a cash crop, but I didn't know about the substantive impact on teenage suicide.

Told 'em that. You hate to discourage anyone who comes in with an idea for what they think the Indians should do. You don't want to turn off their enthusiasm, nor turn away whatever energy and resources they have to offer. We're prideful, but not that prideful.

"You might be able to make a small impact," I told them later, here at the house, in between games of chess, coffee, and some pretty good peji they brought up with them from Colorado. "But I doubt if you'll be able to make a big splash."

We'll see. Turns out they connected with the guys from Porcupine. Hundred and fifty people up there with gardens. They're gonna give it a try.

Anyway, Tom yanked La Roja out of the muck, we sparked up the fire around sundown, and went into the sweat lodge with those guys—Archie (the chess player); Dave, a lawyer who was here in the 70s during Wounded Knee II; and Rusty, Archie's wife, I think. Good people. Wanted to do something in a positive way. They said they really liked the sweat lodge.

"The Old Man took it easy on us," said Tom later here at the house, slapping his chest shirt pockets absentmindedly searching for his Marlboros, looking around.

"Took it easy?" asked Dave. "You say he took it easy?"

Yeah. Hot fire. Ash wood. La Roja sat out behind the woodpile . . . home . . . resting . . . black muck caked all over her tires.

The Transformation of
Betsy

The Reservationization of
Dave Glover's Cadillac

Betsy sat in the garage in Lincoln, Nebraska, for two years, just waiting. All of Dad's cars were "Betsy."

This one was a 1986 Bing cherry Fleetwood Cadillac in prime condition—the kind you see octogenarians driving around, real slow.

Dad drove it until he was broadsided by an Asian lady at an intersection in Lincoln after he ran through a stoplight. He later insisted the light was green. Then one day during a visit down there, out of the blue, he said, "I think my driving days are just about over."

Just about. After getting Betsy repaired, he continued to drive around town, taking Mom out to dinner or the grocery store. Then, suddenly, he just quit driving. The car sat there until he died, and then sat there another two years. Mom didn't drive, my sister was somewhere in Australia, and we didn't need it since we already had two running cars.

Didn't need it until the car we were driving made one too many trips into the high country of Colorado and blew its engine, the turbocharger going bananas at nine thousand feet. Coasted down through Denver and into a Park 'n Ride, where we left it, hoping someone might steal it. Shortly thereafter, I made a trip to Lincoln, and returned to the rez with Betsy. Didn't want to turn her into a rez-mobile. It just happened.

The first thing to go was those fancy hubcaps with the spokes. The gumbo gets all compacted in and around the wheels and makes the car shimmy wayyyyy out of balance, and the steering wheel shakes until it smooths back out at about 140 mph. So those hubcaps had to go. No use in putting them back on. They're in the trunk.

Next thing was a cracked windshield—not from the rocks on Slim Buttes Road being flipped onto the windshield by a passing car, as you might expect, but from a startled prairie hen that, unfortunately for us both, launched itself across the highway south of Rapid City as I was headed north at 70 mph. I didn't stop for the hen, it happened so suddenly. I think what I said, after realizing what happened with the bird flailing behind me in the rearview mirror in a blur of feathers, was, "SON OF A BITCH!"

Had to let it go. No, not the bird. The bird was dead. Let the windshield go. Still driving it "as is." Cracked.

You can drive with a cracked windshield on the rez. No problem. You'll never be stopped. You can drive without taillights, too. Or a license. Or headlights. People are poor. Reservation cops know that. You can drive without a lot of stuff up here that will get you stopped almost immediately, off the rez.

So, there's the cracked windshield. Then the glove box latch mysteriously got busted, so to keep it from constantly flipping down, I stuck some duct tape (what else?) on it to keep it closed. Used more duct tape on the armrests after some small child picked away at the leather.

About the same time, the trunk latch mysteriously got broken when Betsy got loaned out to Tom Cook and Tom Ballanco (bad combo) for a one-day trip to Manderson. Besides Tom, the only other person to drive Betsy was Milo Yellow Hair, who took her to Denver for a flight out of DIA.

I told him my pat response when he asked. "There's only two people who drive Betsy—me and Dad—and Pop hasn't driven her since 1996." But Milo didn't want to take the shuttle coach to Denver—a long, tedious, six-hour bummer of a ride—and he had a hundred bucks.

"Well, okay," I told him. "But drive her like Dad would."

He did, he said. When Milo came back, he said there was a shimmy in the front end . . . but it smoothed back out at about 140.

The Transformation of Betsy   19

That was three sets of struts ago. "Slim Buttes Road," said the mechanic, shaking his head and pressing his lips into a grim line. "That's the third set of struts I've put on this car in TWO YEARS," I told him. He just shrugged and said, "Slim Buttes Road."

It didn't make sense until one evening when Tom Ballanco laughingly told those assembled here that with Tom Cook at the wheel they "went airborne" in Betsy at seventy miles per hour over the Big Dip, a fifty-foot crevasse south of here on Slim Buttes Road, that will tear up an oil pan or undercarriage upon impact if crossed at any faster than thirty miles per hour.

"You should have seen us," said Tom B. "WA-WOOOM."

Yeah. I could picture it.

So, besides all this other stuff, there's the power radio antenna that's broken in the up position (fortunately). Auto pilot . . . cruise control . . . has long since not worked, and the driver's seat won't stay up without the board and plastic soap bucket behind it, making it a tight squeeze for any more than two Indians in the back.

"Hey," said Wes one day, pointing at the Caddy. "This one is starting to look like a rezmobile."

And so it is. That inner liner on the roof? The wind got under it one day and started it billowing and ballooning out. And I sunk one thousand bucks into the rear air shocks at a garage out in Washington State where the mechanics failed to re-assemble all the parts. All the extra stuff was in the trunk. Gave me one of those long-ass printouts you get from a lady behind a computer terminal who doesn't have grease on her hands or know shit from Shinola about the actual work that was done on your car.

"Nine hundred and what?" Screw it. Might as well call it a thousand bucks, huh lady?

But that's okay, because there was one year there, maybe 1999, that Betsy didn't ask for a dime. Just gas and oil. Gas and oil.

"Just change the oil regularly," Dad said.

"Come out here," he said one day, motioning toward the garage, where Betsy sat quiet, waxed, and polished. "I want to show you something."

We went out into the garage and he popped the hood. "Just listen to that," he said, smiling at me with twinkling eyes and looking for my reaction to the engine, clean as a whistle, purring like a kitten. You could hardly tell it was running.

Jesus on the Rez

If you were to ask, "Is Jesus on the Rez?" the answer would be, "Sure. He's here." Stayed here the other night.

Slept on the couch.

He came over this way sometime about the eighteenth century, I think, maybe earlier, when somebody's brother left the monastery in France to tell the folks over this way all about Jesus. Father so-and-so, one of the "Black Robes." Up until that time, The People thought they were okay. They'd never heard of the devil.

For additional details (about the devil), do an online search for "Moravian Massacre."

They still have Jesus up here to this day. Never left, I guess. They have regular Jesus, like Jesus Christ of Latter-day Saints, and Church of Christ, and all those other denominations, "functioning primarily as burial societies," Tom says. And the cross fire branch of the Native American Church has Jesus in their ceremonies, right up there with King Peyote, with the button sitting right on top of the Bible throughout the service. Throughout the night, people will occasionally sing beautiful Jesus peyote songs. In the morning, someone might rise and say a few words about a line of scripture, or Jesus, especially on Easter.

Brother Tom says that's because they had to cover their behinds back in the day when they were busting peyote ceremonies. So when they brought Jesus in there, He gave 'em that protection.

And then again, you got Jesus riding right there on the dashboard. Wallet size. Standard head and shoulder shot—highlight on the forehead—some back-lighting. Looks brown, but has Caucasian features.

But that's okay. It's okay with me, and it's okay with Jesus. As they say on the crew, "itdon'tmattertojesus!"

Picked Him up at a yard sale in Colorado, along with another small "Jesus at the Gate." Two for fifty cents. So, I'm thinking, "Not Bad. Hmmm?" A quarter each. So, with Him riding there, you know, you look over and you see Jesus there in His molded plastic frame, riding along with everybody, and you think, "Jesus is riding with US." It's really comforting. Especially at night when a South Dakota cop might come up and shine his flashlight over your shoulder. First thing he's gonna see is Jesus, sitting right up there on the dash. Comforting.

A lot of people up here like Him. He helps out a lot of people.

Well, no. I've never seen Him in person, but—you know. You know what they say—you know—like, He's always with us?

Hearing the Silence

A friend from New York said, upon her return home, that out here one can "hear the silence." It's true. You can hear the clouds. At night, you can hear the constellations.

You can expect that from someone from who works in Manhattan, but even people from the busy metropolis of Pine Ridge Village who come visit out here also remark about how quiet it is.

"Man, it's quiet out here," they say, standing on the deck and gazing eastward toward Maki Zita.

Every evening, just around sunset, those coyotes down by the river to the east of here get stirred up and begin sounding off with a chorus . . . no, it's not a chorus . . . a cacophony of yelps, calls, and howls that builds into a symphonic crescendo and then cascades into a few isolated, melancholic wails. Everybody around the fire just listens. They don't say anything. Sometimes when the coyotes are so close—I mean, right down there!—they can give you goose bumps . . . give you the yim yams. Makes an Indian want to ease up closer to the fire.

From here you can hear someone coming down Slim Buttes Road, a mile away. "Here comes someone," someone around the fire will say, looking up. It's so quiet, you can even hear when they leave their house.

You hear the wind out here. And the messages in the wind. When all the noise gets quieted down, other things, finer impressions, filter through, opening up avenues of communication or sensitivity that were overwhelmed by the noise. Just listening to the wind, I guess.

Our friend from Kentucky, the hired assassin who was here to exterminate the mice in our greenhouse, stood out back in the blackness of a reservation midnight. "May-an, is it quaat out here," he said, gazing in awe upon the aurora borealis for the first time in his life.

You hear the birds' songs. Finches, meadowlarks, robins, sparrows, and grouse. You can hear their flight. You could hear that eagle up there, circling way overhead. You hear the night birds. Funny, unidentifiable sounds. Nighthawks, owls, and mockingbirds, they say.

You can hear when the old men are about to arrive for ceremony in ten minutes. "We don't need to call them again. They're on their way."

They say that our hearing begins to fail as we age, but it seems to me, when people come here from the "outside world" . . . and some days, the outside world is the reservation line; other days, it's my skin . . . that they seem to be talking really, really loud, like a stage voice, trying to reach that person in the last row.

The people around here aren't loud, especially the old folks. They talk in whispers, and you really have to pay attention.

It's so quiet, you can hear the low hum of the earth turning, churning out a symbiotic electrical exchange with our solar system and the cosmos. You can even hear what that person is thinking . . . from wayyyyyyy over there. You can hear them dialing your number, and you greet them by name when you answer. Sometimes not.

But you can do that over there where you are, too, huh? "I knew it was you," you say when you pick up the phone. Yeah. Everybody does that. That can happen anywhere, and it probably has nothing to do with silence. Probably more of an intuition thing.

And that part up there about hearing the earth turn? Ahhhhh, that's bullshit. It looked good in writing, but it's not accurate. You can't hear the earth turn. You feel it.

People Rolling

Through

You see a lot of people rolling through this reservation. They come here with various motives. Some want to see if we still live in tipis. Some want to "help the Indians." Some want an Indian name. Some want to be adopted into the tribe. Some just want to take some photographs. Some want to donate their time.

Some want to see the Badlands. Some want to visit Wounded Knee. Some want to tell you how guilty they feel. Some want to tell you their great-grandmother was a Cherokee princess.

Some people may want to come to ceremonies, while others want to go to the casino. Some want to eat peyote, and others want to smoke a "peace pipe." Some are looking for a medicine man, and some are looking for Indian artwork. Some are on vacation with their parents, who want to do some of these things and brought the kids along, too. There's one thing these folks all have in common—they want something.

A lady from a Japanese TV production company called and wanted to come here and film somebody making traditional food. Another documentary crew from New York just left. A film crew from Germany is here now. Another crew from England was here last summer. And all of this is just down here in our little corner of the rez.

And besides all of the paid film crews from around the world who seem to have a fascination with Indian America, there's all these independents running around with their equipment and preconceived ideas about what they thought they wanted when they first arrived that's all changed now since reality didn't match up with what they thought they wanted before they left.

There's church groups, donors, scenic bus-line tours, and teams of working volunteers and academics who come to the reservation. There's Hollywoods, and famous names, and The Pres hisself was here, with ALL THAT accompanying a presidential photo op in a headdress. I didn't go. Too much feds. Too much guys on rooftops with too much scopes and guns. Avoided Pine Ridge Village like the plague and read about it in the paper. The Pres said something to the effect of, "We're gonna do something."

The President announced that Pine Ridge was to become an "empowerment zone," and all kinds of good things that The People are still waiting for were going to happen. The People were going to be empowered.

Sounded good. Made for good copy at the time and a good photo op— Clinton in a headdress.

"There's sixty-four nonprofits operating programs on Pine Ridge," said Frank, a former field director for one of those organizations whose mission is to help the Indians. They do. They help. Frank quit. After about a dozen years of frustration, he quit and went off to fight fires somewhere in the Great Northwest.

Literally. Funny, huh? Funny, because that's what he was doing here. He quit because he never got to put any out.

Folks come here for all kinds of reasons.

"I'm just passing through . . . I'm on my way to California . . . I'm only going to be here today and tomorrow . . . and I was wondering . . . could you give me an Indian name?" she asked.

"Yes. You're an idiot."

A guy who didn't know any better, a part-Cherokee guy in Lincoln, Nebraska, asked Loren Black Elk, "Do you think if I go up there, I could get adopted into the tribe?"

Loren cast him a quick glance and looked away, gazing off into the distance while taking a long draw off the cigarette he was smoking. "You've got to do something, first," he told him.

Missing the point, the man asked, "What have I got to do?"

Slightly exasperated with the guy's naïveté, Loren said, "You've got to do something for The People, first. You can't just go in and sign some papers and get adopted into the tribe."

Everybody wants something. That fellow wanted to tell people he'd been adopted into the tribe. There are people out there who seem to want to tell their friends they've been adopted into this or that tribe. And who wouldn't? Everybody needs an Indian friend.

Besides the tour groups and the part-Cherokees, there's people who come here alone, like Jonathan, except he wasn't really alone. After eating a half sack of magic mushrooms he'd picked up in California, he and another guy came here looking for a peyote meeting to attend. Turns out the guy he was with was his baby-sitter.

Just his luck there was a meeting going on that weekend, and they allowed him in there. They said he was entertaining, especially to the little kids, and eventually someone said, "Don't give that guy any more peyote."

Ever listen to someone coming off the downslope of a bad acid trip? He left the peyote meeting over on Rosebud Reservation and came over here, babbling nonstop. I mean, non-freakin-stop—incoherent, disconnected, stream-of-consciousness, sometimes hilarious, off-the-top-of-his-head nonsense that they thought would end when we took him into the sweat lodge in hopes of bringing him back down to earth.

Didn't work. We realized that when he went scrambling over the hot rocks and out the door at the end of the first round. "I gotta get outta here!" he exclaimed after being restrained on his first two attempts by the two guys who were sitting beside him. His brains was still cookin'. If he had gone off the reservation, into Nebraska, they'd have put him in a straightjacket.

And then there's people like Dave, "Just doing the Lord's work" when he drifted into camp down here last summer, coming off a Rainbow Gathering, wearing his sandals, high-water pants, red suspenders, and a bandanna. He wanted to bring "The Word" to the Indians. He had "The Truth," and all of us were pagans, lost in a dark world of illusion.

Uh huh.

That holy man over there, that spiritual elder who's been practicing the traditional ways all his life? He don't know squat. He's been leading every one of us down a dark road of illusion. Quoting scripture, Dave was here to save us and show us the light, claiming he was a tribal member, a member of the "Lost Tribes of Israel," he said. Adopted in, I guess.

Dave moved into the fruit cellar down over the hill in November when the tipi got too unbearable. He could have used some light in that fruit cellar. It was difficult to read scripture down there.

After that second storm lifted, Dave emerged from his dungeon and, since nobody in the neighborhood wanted to adopt him into the tribe, he was given some money and escorted . . . er . . . offered a ride to someplace where they needed some light. The Greyhound bus stop in Cheyenne, Wyoming.

The people around here are mostly tolerant and receptive, but some will tell you straightforward, like a lady friend who said, "Get the fuck out of here," to that Rainbow chick who materialized at a Sun Dance, claiming the "Cosmic Eye" had sent her and that Crazy Horse had appeared in her dream.

I didn't know Crazy Horse had so many incarnations. There's several of him that have rolled through here.

All of ' em white people, so far as I've met. That's okay. Indians believe in dreams. A friend came by the other night and said, "Let's go to the casino. I dreamed I lined up three red sevens on the double diamonds."

Most everybody who comes rolling through here takes back more with them than what they brought.

Some people build a house, or work in the gardens, or paint a house for an elder, or do some other type of constructive work, and maybe take in a powwow before going back to wherever it is they call home.

But Indians are generous people. You're always going to go back with more than you've given, even if you weren't given anything. Don't wait for the star quilt. Don't wait for an eagle feather. Don't wait to be adopted into the tribe.

A Volatile Mix

We had just exited the sweat lodge on the reservation after a good, two-hour sweat, coming out just before midnight, and were headed into Chadron in a caravan of trucks. Sun Dance was only one week away, and we had been preparing all year. It was going to be our second year in the canyon at the Wild Horse Sanctuary—our second year toward the fulfillment of a four-year commitment.

Billy and Wes, who danced with us the first year, weren't with us that night because they had decided to go out drinking with two other nephews, snagging a couple of cases in Chadron. The four of them were on their way back to the reservation in two trucks when Billy went wide in one of the turns on loose gravel and went off the left shoulder, flipping the truck.

Billy managed to free himself from the cab. Mike was trapped, his upper torso clothespinned between the cab and its collapsed roof. His chest was crushed. He lay face down in the dirt. He was dead.

We drove right up on one of our own work crews, stunned and staggering drunk and crying out Mike's name. They kicked at the truck and beat it with their fists. They were making a drunken, futile effort with a handyman jack to lift the truck to pull Mike free. Billy was walking around in a daze, holding his shoulder.

All the people from the sweat arrived and trained their headlights on the accident scene. In a frenzy of activity, people sped off to make calls that resulted in the arrival of an ambulance; the sheriff; the fire department with the hydraulic jaws to peel open the cab; Mike's family; and the coroner.

A lot of men arrived. Men driving fire trucks and rescue equipment that illuminated the wreck scene with their spotlights. County and state cops. Reservation police. A photographer. The coroner. They put a sheet over his body so his mother and sister's last memory of him wouldn't be him lying there.

People were trying to console Billy in one of our trucks. He would soon face the inevitable interrogation by law enforcement. Wes was sitting nearby, crying, his head between his knees. He looked up again and again in disbelief, then slumped back down. The nephews were . . . I don't know where they went.

They took Billy to the hospital for his dislocated shoulder, broken ribs, and bruised chest. Those other guys got off lucky not being charged and went home to sober up and think about a day they'd like to turn back in time. A cop showed up at Billy's hospital bed, read him his rights, and charged him with vehicular homicide.

Two of those guys were Sun Dancers. Billy was a pipe carrier. They say you must be careful with the pipe, or it can hurt you. It was with the rest of Billy's belongings in the back of the truck, before it flipped.

Along with the two cases, one of them full of empties.

"Look here," I said to Tom as we later tried to determine exactly what happened. "This tells a story, doesn't it?" Up on the road, you could see where the truck went off into the grass, hit the embankment, and rolled. Laid out in a straight line were tools, empty beer bottles, Billy's clothes, a deer rifle, his ceremonial items, his pipe lying in the grass, and more beer bottles leading right up to the overturned truck, and Mike.

Tree Day

"Tree Day" is usually the day before the Dance, unless you're Tom Cook, and then it gets put off until the very last minute and you have to go out and find a tree so your Dance can start.

My experience is limited to just a few dances, so I'm not fully acquainted with the procedures of the forty-three or so Sun Dances that take place on the reservation . . . yeah . . . THAT many . . . but, I think you're supposed to go out the year before and lay down prayers and tobacco for the tree you've selected. But as Tom would say, "itdon'tmattertojesus."

Of course, there are many who would say that strict traditional protocols should be observed in all the ceremonies. Others are more relaxed about it. Over here they do it this way . . . over there they do it like that. Everybody's right. "No, they're not doing it right. Their prayers will never be heard," Tom says jokingly about the hypothetical "others."

Although at their core, the ceremonial protocols, songs, and "ways" are the same, in practice they differ from one tiospaye to another, passed down the line by the headmen of those families. Each tiospaye has their own "chiefs," something that was difficult for Europeans to understand ("Who's the Chief?") and what makes governance under the BIA (Bureau of Indian Affairs) difficult to this day.

31

And what's "traditional?" The Old Man looks at many of the procedures and accoutrements accompanying the Dance and says, "They just started doing that yesterday."

"Back in the 'Early Days,'" he said, "only the old men used to dance. Down there in the 'old Sun Dance grounds' (in Pine Ridge Village) is where they used to have it. One Dance," he said. "Just one Dance. There'd be only eight or ten or twelve guys. All old men."

And they say that women never danced. Just the men. And women didn't pierce. They went through childbirth, so they didn't need to, they say. And women didn't go into the sweat. They purify themselves each month, they say. Just the men needed to sweat. But then . . . that person's grandmother over there says . . .

So now, you've got all these things going on . . . women piercing . . . Dances run like "a three-ring circus," everybody says . . . white folks dancing and carrying pipes . . . and a lot of stuff that's not "traditional," whatever that means to the Cherokee princess. It's okay over there . . . but not okay over there. People bitch about it, or accept it. Can everybody be right?

So, over here, we wait until the last minute to get the tree. Last year's tree? It's still up. Over there, they take it down. Down there, they use a live tree. Over here, it's still up. Hundreds of tiny red, white, black, and yellow tobacco prayer ties brought by the people are wrapped around its trunk. It sways magnificently in the wind, all its leaves long since fallen. The faded prayer flags of the dancers flow from the upper branches. Ropes from the dancers hang from the limbs and are wound and twisted from a year's wind.

An ancient eagle feather is still fluttering up there, along with the buffalo and man effigies and the conch Larue said we should put up there for the water. It's beautiful. Magnificent. They're gonna cut it down with a chainsaw.

They're gonna drag it from the arbor, dump it over there, and burn all those ties in this year's fire. They'll remove the protruding stump from its post-hole-digger-length hole with a handyman jack, and get ready at the last minute for the new tree that's going to arrive any minute now.

The entire camp goes out to get the tree, driving in a long caravan of cars and trucks behind the trailer that will bring the tree back to camp. People are encouraged to be there for tree day, because it's a ceremony in and of itself . . . really something you don't want to miss. The fireman stays with the fire. Everybody else goes.

On location, prayers are made and songs are sung around the tree. Ropes are secured to it and laced through the limbs of an adjacent tree to keep it from crashing down. It's not supposed to touch the ground. The people are supposed to catch it . . . support it.

Four virgins, four little girls are selected from the crowd to deliver the first four axe blows. Someone will announce their names and tell everyone why they were selected. When those little girls strike the tree, the people, all in unison, say, "Aho!"

After those little girls, Tom, the lead dancer over at the canyon, strikes it four times. The men dancers all line up and each strike it four times, until it's cut through. As the tree is gently lowered into the arms of The People, some of the women may vocalize that high-pitched tremolo, "li li li li li li li li li," an ancient expression to encourage the warriors.

Right then, you can get goose bumps. It's a magical moment, one of many that will continue through the Dance. The ceremony has begun.

The People carry the tree to the trailer, and usually the young boys will ride back there among the branches. They trim it up a bit and secure it so the branches don't drag on the ground. Then everyone gets back into their cars, lines up behind the tree, and begins the caravan back to camp, stopping four times to pray briefly along the way.

When the tree arrives at the camp, it's lined up with the east "door," or opening of the arbor. All the people pull their cars around the arbor and train their headlights toward the center of the arbor. The fireman has the fire going good.

Then, and it seems to take forever, the men bring the tree into the arbor, accompanied by a special song. It's a high-energy moment, and the guys are talking and wrestling with the shifting weight of the tree. They advance toward the hole and stop just short of putting it in. Then Loretta, wife of our lead dancer Tom, puts the sacred food and water in the bottom of the hole.

It might be then, or maybe before the sacred food goes in, that all The People bring all their prayer ties that they've made . . . sometimes hundreds of them . . . and wrap them around the trunk of the tree. The dancers tie their four long, red, white, black, and yellow cloth prayer flags to the upper branches; they then tie their ropes securely on the strongest limbs. "Tie a good knot," they might say. "You don't want it coming loose," they might say, reminding each other of the piercing they're gonna have to go through later, like the morbid humor of guys going into combat. Sort of an anxious, uneasy moment, right then.

The eagle feather, effigies, and conch are tied to the branches. Then with all the people under the arbor, the tree is guided into the hole, and the men dancers pull it upright, the whole camp erupting with whoops and joy. While the tree is being secured and tamped into the ground, the men dancers stake down their ropes, and the sacred food and water, prepared in quantity, is given out to everybody.

Once the tree is in place, the people exit the arbor and get ready for the Dance to begin the next day, going off to the Main Camp. The men and women dancers remain on the arbor grounds, where they'll stay for four days in separate tipis. People gather around the fire. Some of the dancers remain out there in the dark, fiddling around with their ropes. The tree is beautiful, alive, its leaves talking in the wind.

At the Dance

It was Day Four. One last afternoon of dancing, followed by one last sweat lodge, then we could all go to the feast. We could have water. There'd be watermelon. They'd have fruit. Salmon. Buffalo meat. Potato salad. Lemonade. Strawberries. Fry bread. Jell-o. Greek salad. Rice. Pepsi. Tuna salad. Coffee. Water. Everything. Everything. We just had to get through that last day.

By the fourth day, we'd been joined by more dancers who danced for just the last day, so the arbor was filled up with forty-six dancers, about twice as many as Day One. You can do that. You can dance for as many days as you like. You don't have to dance all four days. You don't have to pierce. You don't have to pull the skulls. You don't have to hang from the tree. You don't have to fast. You don't have to go without water. You don't have to be there at all.

The tree stood elegantly in the middle of the Sun Dance arbor, its trunk wrapped with colored tobacco prayer ties. Foot-long red, white, black, and yellow tobacco prayer flags of the dancers fluttered from the branches. A sea conch clunked against an upper branch where it hung suspended by a piece of rope. An eagle feather played on the breeze among the leaves.

The tree had withstood the fierce winds that blew through camp on Day Two and uprooted the women dancers' tipi. Its limbs now swayed magnificently in the gentle breeze that drifted across the canyon and caressed the hundred or so spectators surrounding the arbor up on the rim of the canyon overlooking the Cheyenne River. A powerful and breathtakingly beautiful spot.

Our skin was parched. The dancers were sunburnt and red—Indians and Anglos alike. Our tongues were swollen. Few had the energy to force air through their eagle-bone whistles. Nobody had any spit left.

It was a long round. Afternoon of the fourth day. People had been piercing throughout the day, and that made the rounds exceptionally long. After each round, we plodded and dragged ourselves from the arbor. A twenty-minute rest in the shade . . . a cigarette . . . time for the singers to get a drink and catch their breath . . . and then back into the arbor for another round. It was almost over.

Most of the men had pierced and had crusty rivulets of dried blood running down their chests, with the holes patched over with sage or tobacco. One over-weight fourteen-year-old had passed out in the unforgiving sun. The two eight-year-old nephews of our intercessor pierced this year and drew victory whoops from the dancers and audience when they made their warriors run around the circle. Raymando had danced with us for three years and now looked triumphant as he made the circle. Poor little Wambli had tears in his eyes. There was only one dancer remaining to pierce. It was almost over. Nonkwa wanted to hang from the tree.

Nonkwa, a dark-skinned young man with a Mohawk haircut and narrow, hawk-like features, came to the Dance with a dozen or so other Mohawks from New York, some of whom danced while others sat in on the drum under the arbor and helped sing. They were our "nephews," and were there by virtue of our lead dancer, Tom Cook, a New York Mohawk. We were otherwise in a sea of Lakota Indians, old and young, with the other half of the Dance group and audience composed of whites. No Cherokees. No Wannabees. People came as who they were.

Tom B., Woody Harrelson's California attorney, had hung from the tree earlier in the round for his second straight year and was a hard act to follow. When we hoisted him up, he spun a few times, then dropped back to the ground. No thanks. Not for me. I didn't need to do that. Woody, dancing on my left, said he didn't want any parts of it either but had gained a new respect for lawyers—at least *this* lawyer. Mike Afraid Of Bear and I had pierced on the second day, getting it over with and making room for people on the last day when there'd be a logjam and long rounds. Actually, I was motivated by the watermelon.

I was with about four other dancers holding a heavy log onto which was tied a long rope that draped over a horizontal log lashed to the Y in the tree. Nonkwa danced forward and lay down on the buffalo robe on his face. He was going to have them pierce him in the back. AIIIIIEEEEEE. We kept dancing. He didn't stir when they ran the scalpel and pegs through his scapulas.

The crowd whooped when they jerked him to his feet and hooked him up to the rope. Then they signaled us to haul him up. When we pulled him off the ground, you could see the initial pain hit him as his body weight hung from the skin of his shoulder blades. He reacted with a shudder, then spun slowly, fifteen feet in the air, an eagle wing in each hand.

He spun and embraced the tree, hugging it, praying for a moment, then kicked free and spun back into the open air, waving the eagle wing fans. He was flying! Flying!

He flew in a slow arc back to the tree and embraced it again. He held it there for a moment, then, kicking free, he spun back into the air, swinging from the skin of his back. He began dancing, then running in the air. Dancing again to the beat of the drum. We stood there, aghast, dumfounded at the spectacle.

Nonkwa circled in the air and back to the tree. He embraced it again, then kicked free. It looked like he was enjoying it now. He spun outward and fanned the entire audience with the eagle wing fans as he made a slow arc, the energy of the fans rippling off the wing feathers like heat waves, cascading onto everyone there. Waves crashed into our chests, as if we were standing armpit-deep in the ocean.

Tears rolled down the faces of some of the women. Little kids stood wide-eyes in amazement, their arms hanging limply at their sides. Some of us weren't breathing. Old people wept. Others stood, mouths gaping. Many of the dancers had stopped dancing, and just stood there, frozen, awestruck. The drum seemed muffled and very far away. Time stopped.

Nonkwa spun back to the tree once again. He embraced it again with his arms wrapped around it, the eagle wings crisscrossed in his hands. He kicked free and spun outward, doing an "Incredible Hulk" imitation—the kind you see pro wrestlers and bodybuilders do when striking a muscle pose. "AAAR-RRRGGGHHHHH," he screamed to the audience as he spun slowly. "AAAAAAARRRRRGGGGGHHHHHH." He flexed himself with the wings in his hands. "AAAAAARRRRRGGGGGHHHHHHHH." The sound was coming from somewhere . . . somewhere deep within his guts . . . a combination of pain, fortitude, and the strength of spirit overcoming pain. The strength of spirit.

"AAAAAAARRRRRRGGGGGHHHHHHHH."

Everybody was absolutely spellbound. Then quiet settled over the grounds. Nonkwa went limp. "I'm done now, Uncle," he said to Tom, who stood at the base of the tree. Then, just as Tom moved to grab Nonkwa's legs to break him free with their combined weight, Nonkwa was released and dropped to the ground, landing on his feet.

Slim Buttes Road

Four flat tires in two weeks has provided the inspiration to finally write about this road. Simply put, Slim Buttes Road is a killer. "That's gotta be one of the worst roads in America," laughed Mike down at Hills Tire in Chadron as he soaped the tire, looking for bubbles.

"Ahhhhh. There it is," he said. "Looks like another rock puncture."

That's one nail and three rock punctures in two weeks.

"You oughta stay off of it," said Mike, just like a doctor might say, as he removed the tire from the rim with the shop's hydraulic tire machine. "Or go around."

"I can't stay off of it, unless I stay home. I live right in the middle of it."

"They must've just graded it," he said. "You're the fourth person in here today with a flat from that road."

Slim Buttes Road runs north to south for thirty-two miles, connecting Highway 18, which runs past Oglala, to Highway 20, running through Chardon. The upper part of the road is partially paved to the reservation line, then it turns to gravel for the last twenty miles into Chadron.

Headed north, out of my mile-long, rutted driveway, the road is at its worst. Traffic has to slow to five miles per hour to negotiate the half mile long gauntlet of broken pavement and potholes. Any faster, and you're asking for bent tie-rods, broken axles, busted springs, or screwed-up struts. At the very least, you'll need a realignment, as my daughter discovered. "This road really sucks," she said.

Right through here there's a permanent passenger's side tire trail on the shoulder, where everyone drives off the road to avoid the road. Also, right along this particular strip, people headed north drive straight up the left-hand side, which is more negotiable than the right. You just pray there isn't someone coming the other way over the hill.

Only person I've seen take it faster than five miles per hour was Bo Davis, who at the time was out-running the police. From the house we could hear the sirens, first headed south, and then, about fifteen minutes later, back north.

"He must've been going over a hundred miles an hour when he went around me," said the Old Man, describing the chase to us that night around the sweat lodge fire. "Police right on his ass. I said, 'Well I'll be damned. That's Bo Davis.'"

Bo eventually wrecked the car down by the river and got away on foot, but they arrested him later in the Sioux Nation parking lot in Pine Ridge.

"I knew they couldn't catch me once I got to the river," laughed Bo later. "I know that river bottom like the back of my hand."

Just north of the gauntlet and before the T junction that runs east into Pine Ridge, there's a series of five deep, strut-busting potholes that are possible to avoid if you know where they are. Straddle . . . to the right . . . to the right . . . straddle . . . straddle. If you hit one of these sinkholes dead-on, your car will need to go to the shop. It's enough to rattle the fillings in your teeth or make your headlights pop out, like the old Donald Duck cartoons when Donald wraps his jalopy around a lightpole and the eyeball headlights pop out on coiled springs.

After swerving around the series of deadly potholes, the road goes up and over a hill by the church and through a winding stretch of a half dozen roller-coaster dips, produced from repeated freezing and thawing, that need to be taken at less than forty miles per hour. Any faster and your car will bottom out, after the springs have been fully extended while the car is airborne, then come crashing down, risking neck injury to your occupants when they hit their heads against the roof.

There are long, permanent, white parallel scars on the black asphalt road surface at the point where innumerable drain plug bolts on oil pans have scored the pavement.

I was with a redhead from Washington one time who ran this stretch at fifty in a rental car, lifting everyone out of the seats. "You'd better slow down," I said after we hit the first dip, bracing my hand against the roof to hold myself in the seat.

Instead, with pure devilish delight in her eyes, she laughed and tromped down on the accelerator, not being the kind of woman who liked being told what to do. As we hit the dips, the two kids in the back hollered out, "WHEEEEEEEE," as they were lifted out of their seats.

The car came crunching down after each of the six dips, scraping the spoiler and entire undercarriage of the car. I winced, while she and the kids just laughed. Like I said, she was driving a rental.

After the dips and past the dirt cut-across (also known as "the Gaza Strip" because of the danger of getting mired down around the river, and the occasional gunfire) connecting the Pine Ridge road, you pass the T intersection going into Pine Ridge, and the rest of the road north to Oglala is gravel again.

That portion of the road is rough, runs like a washboard, and could be the road to Baghdad, looking like something that a convoy went down and suffered air and artillery strikes. There's three or four really bad craters you have to swerve around or go down into and back up the other side. Along through there you frequently see people stopped on the roadside, blinkers on.

The road running north from here to Oglala—that's the good part. Running south to Chadron, it's worse.

The first thing you encounter heading south, about a mile from here, where the road crosses a creek, is a huge dip . . . a crevasse. If you hit this dip any faster than thirty miles per hour, you're going to have undercarriage damage. Southbound, you're going to slam into the other side of the crater. Northbound, you're for sure going airborne.

Tom Cook, in a momentary lapse of awareness while in a hurry and having his mind somewhere ahead of where he was, like at a meeting at Porcupine or Wounded Knee, took my Cadillac and Tom Ballanco over the dip at seventy. I needed new struts after that ride. The third set I've put on my car because of Slim Buttes Road.

Further south of the Dip, which, incidentally, is marked, there's more patches of broken pavement for three miles, and a speed bump running the full width of the road that can chip your teeth if you hit it going more than fifty. Then you cross the auto gate, or cattle guard, cross the rez line, and you're in Nebraska. From there to Chadron, it's all gravel. Southbound, a sign says to watch for cattle on the road. Northbound says, "Welcome to Pine Ridge."

They say there were a couple of girls killed there at the reservation line when they hit the cattle guard, and just north of there, two "Why Die?" signs mark the spot where a couple of other guys died a few years back. They laid in the ditch undiscovered for months, until one day Bo Davis heard a car horn blowing constantly throughout the night. They went out there the next morning and found the wreck and decomposed bodies.

South of the cattle guard, across the line into Nebraska, the unfenced land allows those black angus cows right onto the road, so you have to be extra careful, especially on dark and rainy nights. I missed one just by inches one night, when at the last moment I realized what was standing in the road. Just a couple of months ago, my neighbor's wife hit one and tore up the front end of their car.

Even in the daytime, when they see you bearing down on them, those cows will stand right in the middle of the road, and won't move until they can read your lips. It's like it takes a really long time for their brains to register that their lives are in danger. Then they get that wide-eyed look and suddenly bolt off the road, always headed in the direction their heads are pointed . . . not like a squirrel or a rabbit . . . so, you can cruise by them at fifty, as long as you point your car toward their ass-end.

On this portion of the road, you can go sixty, seventy, eighty miles an hour in the straight stretches. In the curves, however, of which there are no less than two dozen, half of which are sharp, ninety-degree turns, you've got to slow down to a crawl. Elderly Indians and out-of-staters, like people from Colorado, travel the entire stretch at about thirty-five to forty miles per hour, but the local Indians will run it wide open, sliding and fishtailing in the turns.

If you lose it on the loose gravel in the turns, you're going into the ditch, like Billy did the night they overturned in the blue truck.

In addition to killing people, you'll see roadkill retreads all along the road. There's often mufflers and tailpipes lying in the grass, along with bags of trash, beer bottles and empty cardboard cases, an occasional drive shaft, baby diapers, wheel rims, hubcaps, and once, a refrigerator that didn't make it all the way to the dump.

Apart from the litter and car parts, the land is prettier down that way; that's why it's off the reservation. It's also good grassland for ranchers; another reason why it's valuable enough to be Nebraska, and not the reservation.

Up in this northernmost corner of the state, the land is rolling and expansive, broken by washes filled with elm and gnarly ash trees. Chalky buttes and yellow ochre pine-covered ridges rise out of the ground, stretching for miles. Were it not for the road that requires constant vigilance, the dreamy landscape could lull you to sleep.

Hawks sit atop fence posts, and spotted eagles sometimes soar overhead. Pheasant and grouse flutter across the road. Herds of sleepy-eyed antelopes graze here, and wild turkeys roam the land, especially at the halfway point where the road crosses the White River.

It's there, according to the Old Man, that travelers back in the "early days" would park their teams and wagons under the cool of the cottonwood trees, taking a midday lunch break from the all-day drive into town. "There'd be three or four wagons parked down there," he said. Now the drive takes twenty-five minutes.

It's there, in the S-curve where the road passes across the river, that you can maintain sixty miles an hour, hugging the inside of the curves if you can catch a glimpse of the road ahead through the trees to make sure there's nobody coming the other way. After a short rain and before the road turns snot-slick, the conditions are tacky and excellent for speedy travel, akin to dirt track racing. If there's too much rain, deep ruts are carved into what is commonly referred to as "gumbo," making the travel hazardous, questionable, or impossible. No rain at all, which is the case most of the time, and you send up a rooster tail of dust that can be seen for miles.

Ironically, the worst conditions are right after the road has been graded, removing the washboard effect. You'd think that's when it would be ideal, but contrarily, the grader pulls rocks, wire, glass, and trash from the side of the road and deposits it back on the surface. The loose gravel gets pushed into long rows on either side of the common tire ruts, and running up onto the piles of stone can make your car fishtail or suddenly lurch three feet to the side of the road or put you in the ditch. I've been in it, and so have many others.

Henry went off it in a curve. Milo went off it. Melvin Lee went off down by the river. Wes went off it. And one time during a blizzard, with Tom at the wheel, we spent the night in a snowdrift, along with a couple of the Red Cloud boys, until the next morning when a road grader yanked us out.

Once we came upon an overturned passenger car with the wheels still spinning. The driver, a young Indian woman, was outside, a little dazed. The two oldest of the five kids riding with her were pulling the younger ones from the car. Incredibly, nobody was hurt, not a scratch, but one of the little ones who was old enough to know what had happened was shaking uncontrollably.

The next-to-the-littlest one was laughing. A couple more cars stopped, and the men pushed the car back over on its wheels. The woman loaded the kids back in the car, we pulled her out with our two-ton and a log chain, and away they went.

The necessities for traveling this road are a spare or a doughnut, an air tank, a log chain, five extra gallons of gas, a gallon of water, a flashlight, a jack, and a four-way lug wrench. Oh yeah. Duct tape. Don't leave home without it.

That's one of the good things about this road that you won't experience too much in the rest of America. People will stop to help. Nobody up here is in that much of a hurry. The first time I met Oliver Red Cloud was right there at the rez line. The Old Man was under his car, changing a flat from the freshly graded road.

That's when the rock punctures occur. You may also wonder why they don't use a smaller stone, but these are crushed to about the size of golf balls, with sharp jagged edges that "just *gnaws* at your tires," as Henry Red Cloud says. "Just *gnaws* at 'em."

Four flats in two weeks. After a dozen flats a couple of years ago, I stopped counting. Three sets of struts. Two sets of shocks, tie rods, three transaxles, and a busted windshield. That's just the car. My truck is a whole nuther story.

Serving as a major economic corridor between Pine Ridge and the border town of Chadron, Slim Buttes Road is a vital artery, and on a trip to town, you'll pass several carloads of Indians, coming or going. At any given time, half the clientele of Wal-Mart are Indians. Half of the license plates in the parking lot are from South Dakota.

When Tom got appointed to the Nebraska governor's Commission on Indian Affairs, representing this highly-populated corner of the state, but far removed from the political center of Lincoln, I told him, "If you can accomplish just one thing, why don't you see if you can get Slim Buttes fixed. They'll make you a chief!"

Ain't happened yet.

For as much traffic as there is on it, day and night, it's got to be one of the deadliest and worst high-volume roadways in the nation. As a rule, reservation roads are notoriously bad, but this one is in a class all by itself. If Indians had a wish list, there would probably be a lot of other items at the top, but something you hear the locals say quite often is, "I sure wish they'd fix that road."

Rez Death

Among the many things that distinguish the reservation from the outside world is the way in which death is treated. It happens often and disproportionately up here, relative to the rest of the country. You can die easier and sooner here than anywhere in the nation.

Up here (Pine Ridge Indian Reservation), in this (Lakota) culture, a person gets laid out, embalmed, dressed up, and put in a nice, cushioned, satin-lined casket just like people in the outside world. They have all-night wakes, like other cultures, during which the family receives relatives, friends, and visitors, and people cry, like everywhere. But then, there are some differences.

In the old days, they used to put people up on a burial scaffold—maybe you've seen those paintings of the "departed warrior." But now, they bury people in the ground in the traditional sense. Beyond that, it's quite different.

When you walk in, you know it's Indian. There are star quilts and blankets draped over the casket. On folding tables, usually in a gym or community building, or sometimes in a giant ceremonial tipi, you'll find several large, flat, memorial cakes with a short message, along with the dates of birth and death.

You'll smell sage or cedar and sweet grass burning in an abalone shell. If the person was a warrior, you'll see eagle feathers laid out, along with eagle feather staffs. There will be a traditional sacred pipe laid out that people will smoke later. People will leave things in the casket, like small red tobacco ties, eagle feathers, single cigarettes, and sticks of Big Red chewing gum.

There will be feeds, with fry bread, coffee, and traditional spirit food of corn, meat, and chokecherry wasna, usually prepared by the old women who know how to make it best. Small amounts of any food that is fixed is also left for the spirit of the departed on small paper plates on a table or flat surface that has been established as a makeshift altar.

During the ceremony, a drum group will sing beautifully haunting memorial songs. Tobacco and water might be offered at the gravesite. People might leave things on the grave.

Afterwards, the relatives have a "wiping of the tears" ceremony, consisting of a sweat lodge and maybe burning their black mourning clothes. They might cut their hair as a symbolic gesture of their grief and loss.

For one year the people participate in a "keeping of the spirit," during which time social proscriptions are observed by family members in respect for the departed. For instance, a widow shouldn't go out partying around, dating, or going to powwows and other gala social events.

At the end of the year, the family holds a memorial service, where they "release the spirit" and end their grieving. Closure occurs psychologically for the family and the community. The service can be brief or elaborate, as in the case of the Native American Church members who hold all-night peyote meetings, and are really sad, the peyote magnifying people's emotions. Following the service, there will be another huge feed and a giveaway of all kinds of things that have been purchased, created, and collected by the family over the course of the past year.

As poor as the people are, you'll sometimes see thousands of dollars of gifts given away at one-year memorials. Sometimes they'll give away everything and start all over from scratch. Designated personal items may be given to specific people, telling them that the departed would want them to have it. Sometimes the items are laid out on blankets and people can just come up and take whatever they want.

Lots of star quilts, valued at approximately $450 or more if they're hand stitched, are given away. People give Pendleton and Hudson's Bay blankets, Indian-designed pillows and cushions, towels, baskets, cookware, and all kinds of household things that people can use. Kids get toys, and teenagers get things like tape players.

This giveaway, in addition to the ceremonies and protocols accompanying death in Indian Country, is reflective of the gift of life from the Creator and its formal closure a year following death. And although the person has gone off to the Spirit World, they can still be addressed by the living and, it is believed, remain an influence in the physical world.

— — — — —

Sometimes death occurs in clusters, and people shake their heads and ask what's going on. A member of our Slim Buttes community, Alfred Yellow Horse, Jr., a Vietnam vet and drinker, was killed last week when he stumbled out in front of a car near the just-off-the-rez border town of White Clay, Nebraska. Another young man lost at Russian roulette a few days later. And then, Jun Little died.

Jun, born Wallace Little Jr., was also a Vietnam vet who served with me in helicopter units in Chu Lai, Vietnam. Jun was a door gunner with the gunships. He was also an AIM (American Indian Movement) warrior veteran of the Wounded Knee II takeover in 1973. He pretty much single handedly took over the tribal government building last year in the name of the Grassroots Oyate (people), who ousted and shut down the tribal government.

Although some of the long-winded, high-profile "big" Indians do the talking at public events and news conferences, Jun, from Oglala, was always perceived as a local American Indian Movement leader. He returned home from Vietnam angry about the situation still facing his people. Jun lost an eye and arm in a bomb-making blast back during the years of turmoil that led to Wounded Knee II, earning him the nickname of "The Hook."

Jun had big dreams for his Lakota people, held a true sense of justice, was sober in a sea of drunks, and helped organize the Sacred Hoops Basketball Court Project for the young people in Oglala. Last year, in his sacrifice for the people, Jun tied himself to the Sun Dance tree for four days. He had three or four wives and fifteen kids, and there's a lot of his personal history left obscured. I asked him once why he didn't want to go on a road trip to Colorado, and he said, "Bro, there's nothing out there that I want. My work is here, and I've got my hands full. And besides," he added with a chuckle, "there's a warrant out there for my arrest."

Seeing my friend Jun, the warrior, the outlaw, and "The General," as they called him, laid out there all peaceful with hundreds of people coming around to pay their respects, is what inspired this essay. He survived Vietnam, but fell victim to being an Indian in Indian Country.

About This Food Thing

Everybody eats somebody else. Some life form's gotta die. At least, here on this table, that seems to be one of the primary functions and motivations to sustain life. The most basic of physiological drives.

Gotta eat.

Just what we eat seems to depend heavily upon where we live. In Africa, you might be eating insects. In Asia, street vendors serve up fried grasshoppers on large, flat trays. In England, folks have gone vegetarian, en masse, overnight. In California, the diet is much different from, say Nebraska, or here on the rez.

Pretty much everyone in Nebraska is overweight. Up here on Pine Ridge, where diabetes hits half the population over forty-five, The People eat government commodities from black and white generic cans. Lots of sodium and sugar. And as a result, coupled with the lethargy of unemployment and the welfare-state mentality, a lot of The People are obese. Many of The People believe the government is still trying to exterminate them through the food.

So, the way we look, given a certain genetic predisposition, is a function of what we eat, how much we eat, and our attitude about it.

That aside, until we learn differently, our attitudes about food may be shaped by cultural or family values. Growing up near the banks of the Wabash River, I learned that when somebody showed up at dinnertime, they were an inconvenient pain in the ass.

That attitude about food got reshaped here, where a feast-or-famine mentality prevails. You share whatever you've got. If someone shows up right at dinnertime, you set out another plate. Give 'em some coffee. "The Creator sent that person to your door, so you feed them," Loretta said. "The Creator's looking down, and he sees this house feeding The People, and that's where The People go, so he makes sure this house always has lots of food."

"These people over here," she said, motioning toward the floor with a shake of her hand, "they never put anything out for people, so sometimes their cupboards are empty."

Late one night in a house full of The People, she also said to her husband, "Honey, maybe we should go to bed. These people might want to go home."

The poorest people will make you eat when you stop by. And you can't just jump up . . . in and out. You have to drink a pot of coffee. You can't say, "Sorry, I don't care for any of the artery-blocking, triple-bypass tanega (cow intestines) soup," or whatever. You gotta eat.

My neighbor over there across the road, Sandy, feeds multitudes. Seems to delight in making muffins, cakes, pies, soups, and everything. Even delivers it. Seems to be especially challenged by groups over twenty. "Creative cooking with commodities," she calls it.

At ceremony feeds and feasts, The People bring watecha buckets—containers for leftovers, usually consisting of several large Tupperware containers and one-pound coffee cans.

All of the huge amounts of food are meant to be taken home, so that food and all those blessings get spread out far among the families.

The hosts, or sponsors, don't expect anything to be left over. The People take it all. Even if you don't attend the ceremony, you are often asked to come and eat, and so people do . . . all the time . . . just show up for the meal.

Once during a winter blizzard, Tom and I stopped at Sam and Angie Loud Hawk's on the way home. Sam and Angie, who were later both murdered by their troubled son following a dispute over car keys, had us sit down at their prepared dinner table—big plate of deer meat, mashed potatoes, gravy, and vegetables. The whole family was just ready to sit down, but Angie made the kids go into the TV room until Tom and I ate and finished drinking a pot of coffee with their dad. Then she made us eat seconds.

I looked around. Pictures of the kids and grandkids on the wall. A girl with a cap and gown and diploma.

Sam and Angie's cupboards were full.

Medicine Family

It wasn't until I was trying to explain to Dave (the Yeshua guy who said God told him to come to Pine Ridge) that I realized for myself that this is a medicine family he was trying to convert to his way of thinking.

"Dave," I told him, "you've landed right smack in the middle of a medicine tiospaye. The folks here have withstood five hundred years of onslaught by American values and culture, and yet they still have their language, their culture, and their religion all intact."

Dave kept quoting scripture to us and began a lot of his statements with, "The Bible says . . . "

That got old really quick. Aloysius started calling him "His Holiness" and "My Lord."

"You aren't the first guy to come through here with a Bible," I told him. "As far as I can tell, The People aren't interested in what you're peddling."

He must not have been listening, because there were about sixteen other people around here who were telling him the same thing. Ran off him like water off a duck's back. Where he came from, they didn't use drums in his church.

But here, the people were tolerant, and after all the summer volunteers and campers left, Dave was down there in a tipi. I showed him how to split wood with an axe. Around September, when tipi living became too unbearable, he moved into one of the root cellar containers, and after drifting from house to house in November, it slowly dawned upon him that this wasn't a commune.

He came into the sweat lodge just once. He cried in there, but it's anyone's guess why.

Like Dave, there are a lot of people who come through here, looking for a place to land for awhile. There are empty trailers, shacks, and campers around, if you look. Right now, Lupe and Mike are down over the hill in a motor home, getting on one another's nerves, Lupe said.

Well, it's February, going on March. It's tough here during the winter. That's no secret. South Dakota winters are extreme, relative to Kansas or Missouri. In the winter, there's no people in camp, to speak of. All of the summer volunteers are gone. All of the people coming through are gone. The white women stop coming,* the tipis come down, the kitchen gets closed, and the solar showers are drained. Even the rez dogs stop coming through. Lean, mean months.

But we keep the sweat lodge going. Twice a week. On Wednesdays and Sundays there'll be a group of people assembling around sundown to "take in." A few of the core group of guys will show up to stack the rocks and spark it up. Then the Old Man will show up, and we'll all stand around the fire waiting for Uncle Joe American Horse, the Old Man's first cousin.

"This is a way of life," someone once said about The Ways. So, even in the winter, there are families across the reservation who keep their lodges going. There are Native American Church meetings, house ceremonies, and Yuwipi and Lowanpi ceremonies continuing on by the traditional people.

So, it took some time to figure out the relationships within the family and realize that the folks in the tiospaye are descendants of medicine people. There

— — — — —

*I say this as a joke. One day, when I walked back five miles from where I had been cutting wood and gotten the truck stuck, everyone was here at the house waiting for someone, me I guess, to light the fire. I just didn't feel like it, given my recent hike, and neither did anyone else, so we were all . . . about eight of us . . . sitting here drinking coffee and shooting the shit. Wouldn't you know it—Beatrice and Loretta drive up, wanting to sweat. We sweat twice a week, year round, and usually it's just the guys. But that day, the women wanted to sweat.

"Where's the fire?" they asked.

Someone . . . some foolish man . . . went out and told them, "We've called it off."

I won't say who, but one of those women replied, "The only time you guys want to sweat is when there's white women."

Eeeeeeeeeee. Someone, Tom, I think, went out and lit it up right away. We laugh about it to this day, but at the time, nobody was laughing. It wasn't funny.

are medicine families within communities across the reservation who still preserve The Ways.

And in a given generation of children, maybe only one will be the one who "carries the medicine." The others may turn out to be drunks, Baptists, ordinary people, or incarcerated. Just because a person has "A Name" doesn't necessarily connote a particular spiritual path or commitment.

I could provide some examples, but since this might someday hit print, and I don't want enemies, I just won't say. Don't need to. Ain't necessary.

So after a while, you learn who these folks are. When I first met Larue, he was fixing fry bread in a tiny little shack on land shared by his brothers. Larue was a thirty-five-year peyote "road man," recognized medicine man, and spiritual leader of the Afraid Of Bear tiospaye.

Of the brothers who were living there with him at the time, one was a recluse, one was drinking on and off, and the other was a recluse, too. Tom Cook's father-in-law, Ernest, was Larue's fireman, a job he had all his life, up till then.

"How come you always work this fire and stay outside?" I asked him once after a sweat lodge conducted by Larue.

"Because this is what I do," he said simply.

Ernest went on to tell me that his dad had given each of the boys a job, and the fireman's job was his. Larue was taught to run ceremony, and Steven had the songs. In "Early Days," he said, they used to sing in a group, go to powwows, compose their own songs, and take in peyote meetings all the time.

Steven died, and then Larue, after the second year of the Sun Dance in the canyon. It was his vision to return the Sun Dance to those grounds, and he talked about it a lot until it was realized and fulfilled.

Before he died, Larue gave me his songs, one at a time, over a five-year period, making certain I had them right before giving me another. Sometimes I still hear him singing in my right ear when using his songs. I'm not singing Larue's songs—I'm singing along with him.

Somewhere along the way, Ernest married Beatrice, and they had Loretta, then Poncho, then Nita, then Mike. Beatrice is a bona fide medicine woman, who, as far as I can tell, knows everything. Loretta, too. Then later, and I don't know all the ins and outs, but later, Beatrice married the late Johnny Weasel Bear, he too, a medicine man. They had Aloysius. And as far as I can tell, Aloysius received from his mother the knowledge of everything.

And it's true. Loretta, her mom, and Aloysius are walking encyclopedias of the traditional ways. Nobody seems to dispute that, although they may give you three different explanations of a given topic. You may ask what you may think is a simple question, and they'll give you a half-hour discourse, somewhere in there providing an answer.

So, in addition to learning who's who, and who's cousin is whose, and who's half-brother is whose, one eventually learns just exactly who "The Relatives" are. And among those relatives, one eventually learns who is serious in The Ways, who's just playing, who's drinking, and who's not interested at all.

Lynnette's Memorial

Around here, some days you have no personal agenda. The old folks' agenda is your agenda. Our agenda for the day is simply to carry out the wishes of the elders.

In this case, today, my agenda was to fulfill the requests of Beatrice Weasel Bear, who lives just over the hill. Beatrice is the matriarch of the Afraid of Bear tiospaye in Slim Buttes community—and for that matter, Pine Ridge Reservation. When Beatrice talks—people listen. And, uh . . . like everyone we know, you want to stay on her good side.

For the past year, she has been preparing for Lynnette's one-year memorial, a "releasing of the spirit" ceremony. Lynnette, the granddaughter of Beatrice and Ernest, was killed instantly, along with three others, when the car they were travelling in at one hundred fifteen miles per hour, disintegrated when it came up over a hill and smashed into the back of a parked tow truck, just east of the casino. There's four white crosses out there now.

Lynnette came back from Idaho to live here on Pine Ridge, close to her relatives. She was the daughter of Mike Afraid of Bear, my Sun Dance brother who has danced along side me in the lineup for the past five years—two at Devil's Tower with Charlotte Black Elk and her husband Gerald Clifford, and three in the Canyon at the Wild Horse Sanctuary with Tom and Loretta. Mike and I bonded when we picked up our commitment at the same time five years ago, and have kept each other going when the other started to lag.

Lynnette came home to Pine Ridge, and soon thereafter began drinking.

So this Saturday night, they're having her memorial. In preparation, many things must be "lined out" for her service, an all-night "tipi meeting"— a peyote meeting of the Native American Church.

A cow or buffalo must be slaughtered. Corn, chokecherry and meat wasna, the sacred spiritual foods that will be required for the event, must be made. Beatrice, being renowned for making the best wasnas, had prepared them in advance. They need fry bread and food to feed the people first breakfast, second breakfast, lunch, and then main meal for the multitudes.

Someone needs to make a trip down to the peyote gardens down in South Texas for the "medicine," about a thousand buttons for a meeting, or know someone who knows someone who's got a thousand buttons—"a thousand peyotes" they say around here.

They need a "Road Man," the Native American Church minister who'll conduct the ceremony, and give him about . . . I don't know . . . depends on how far he travels . . . about five hundred bucks, so he and his family, his drummer, cedar man, and fireman can pack up, gas up, and come over here. I don't know who they've asked. Willard, I think. Willard Fool Bull, from Rosebud Reservation, the Sicangus, or "Burned Thighs," just to the east of Pine Ridge.

Sometimes they'll ask a Navajo. Sometimes an Arapahoe Road Man relative from Wyoming. These Native American Church ministers travel far to conduct meetings, sometimes going to Germany, all expenses paid.

You gotta put up a 30-foot tipi. That's a big one. 35-foot poles, the base of which is about the size of a small telephone pole. Takes a half-dozen guys to set the main pole with the 400 pound canvas. No small job.

This past weekend, the relatives were building the shade arbor, "popping the holes" with a post-hole digger for sixteen ash crutches to hold the pine boughs. I was asked to help with the crutches and "stringers," and since I don't loan my chainsaw out to anyone (you just can't do it), I needed to go out with Beatrice's son, Aloysius, a couple of Navajo brothers, and "La Roja Grande," the dump truck, and cut the required trees. Couple three hours work.

And then there's the giveaway. Beatrice's cousin has been over at the "old place" (Beatrice's old home just over the hill) hand-stitching star quilts for two months. Who knows what else they've been accumulating for the past year to give away in Lynnette's honor. All kinds of stuff.

And you wonder, especially during the feed and the giveaway, how these poorest people in America can pull this off. It's just something they do. They've alway done it. Taking care of these spiritual matters is a priority in their lives.

Lynnette's Memorial   55

Lynnette used to come over here some mornings with her dad for coffee when they were in the neighborhood, staying at the old place. She was light-skinned and, I don't know, sort of felt like she didn't fit in so much, she said, but wanted to be around her relatives. Lynnette liked to laugh.

She'd call here sometimes, drunk, asking for her dad, but really wanting more just to talk for fifteen or twenty minutes, wanting to know if anyone cared about her. Shortly before her death, she called and without announcing who she was, disguised her voice and said, "I just wanted to call to inform you that Lynnette Afraid of Bear was killed in a car wreck last night with three other people . . . please tell the relatives."

"Oh NO...oh no...oh no....oh nooooo," I said to the caller.

There was silence on the line for a moment, and then she burst out laughing. "VIC! THIS IS LYNNETTE," she said.

"DON'T DO THAT!" I admonished her. "JESUS, Lynnette! Don't do that!"

She just laaaaaauuuughed.

I told Loretta and Mike about that call. Mike, who sometimes stammers, said, "Hey Brother. She . . . she . . . she must've known. She must've known something."

And after she died, they asked me about it again in Loretta's kitchen, with a lot of the family around. I told the story again. Everyone just sort of looked at the floor. Some of them said softly, "Hmmm."

Rez Dogs

One might wonder what these guys did in a prior lifetime that got them reincarnated as a rez dog. You know when The People are destitute and living in welfare-state poverty, their dogs are gonna have a tough life. Times get hard enough, they could even end up in the soup pot.

Rez dogs don't get to wear bandannas and ride in cars with their owners, like they do down in Colorado. They don't have collars or get spayed or neutered. They get table scraps, fleas, ticks, the mange, and hit by cars. I don't think I've ever witnessed a rez dog get petted by his owner or scratched behind the ears. Christ! You might get something on your hands! They have to wait for someone off the reservation, like a summer volunteer.

Rez dogs are really, really wary of strangers, shying away in wide arcs with that low, distrusting growl that tells you they're not going to let anyone get close enough to kick them in the ribs again. Unless you've got food. Even then, they expect you to throw it. They aren't going to take food out of your hand.

Take food from your hand? It took two months for that vagrant mutt from over the hill to ease up, lean forward on his toenails, stretch his neck out, peel back his lips, and snatch that piece of bread out of my hand with just the ends of his teeth, legs quivering, eyeing me with apprehension the whole time. Then he ran off a safe distance and wolfed it down . . . and looked up in wonder and anticipation for another slice.

Up at Oglala, probably one of the worst places on Earth a dog could be born, a medium-sized black dog lay on the side of the road up by the post office for over a month. His buddies moved around him, past him, not even giving him a sniff . . . going on about their business . . . survival . . . kind of like the 'Nam.

Down this way, a pack of six wild dogs kept daily inspection of a dead skunk in the road, eventually pulling it off to the side, waiting for it to get "just right" . . . waiting for another ceremony when they all hang around, knowing when The People gather like that they're going to eat good.

When I moved in here, I inherited Shunka (which means "dog") and Watecha (which means "leftovers"), a couple of abandoned pups who were both starving and eating from the commodity pile of rusting trash behind the house. Gave 'em both flea collars and worming medicine, and bought dog food . . . watched as they gorged themselves on it, threw up, and kept eating.

Shunka never could get enough to eat, so he supplemented his regular twice-a-day feeding with the rusting commodity pile. He got into something bad . . . had to be beef stew . . . from the pile one day. Got bleary-eyed, locked up, and died. His sister, Watecha, went to Sandy across the road, who really needed some company over there.

Watecha probably thinks she has gone to heaven. Got a rug of her own inside. INSIDE?! WHAT?!

Indians don't let their dogs live inside, usually. Gets regular meals. Got a collar. Gets baths and brushed. Geeeeee.

Gets to go along in the back of the truck. Sometimes she runs the three miles over here, just to say hi.

All the neighbors' dogs come through here, too. About every day they make their rounds. Mongrels, all of them. About ten of 'em from three different houses. That black and white dog hasn't been back since he came into the house and grabbed the whole sack of dog food and was making his way back over to his place with it in his mouth.

Exiting from the greenhouse, I saw this crime in progress, so I yelled at him, chased him, called him all kinds of names until he finally dropped the bag and skedaddled. His buddy, a German Shepherd mix-blood whose grandmother was a Cherokee princess, stood off to the side, watching warily, but obviously starving . . . his legs spread like a sawhorse, his spine swaybacked, his ribs protruding.

"You didn't steal from me, so I'll feed you," I told him, returning with the bag. He seemed to understand and lay down patiently in the driveway until a pan got filled. Then he came over and ate with me standing right there, something he'd never done before, driven by starvation. After he ate, he came up on the porch and let Lupe pull a nickel-sized tick off his muzzle. We talked to him. Afterwards, he glanced back and said thanks, then trotted on over home.

That little brown and black bitch over the hill that looks like a relative to a rat, cranks out a litter about every nine months and has to wait for summer volunteers from New Jersey and Massachusetts to pull the ticks off of her in July. She slinks up to you, ears laid back, rolls over, and exposes her jugular.

Taking opportunistic advantage of my door always being open, she and two of her pups from two different litters came in here one day and took three kinds of cheeses, meat, and two sleeves of saltines right off the table, while I was outside just two hundred yards away sparking up the sweat lodge fire. They approached the house later when I came up to get water. They were all full and fat and round and grinning, happy. All their expressions changed when I angrily told them to "get the hell outta here," and they haven't been back since.

Up in Oglala . . . probably the worst place on Earth a dog could be born . . . the dog of a friend of mine had his nose full of porcupine quills, swollen and oozing. I'd never seen anything quite like that before. "We got a few of 'em with pliers," he said. "And then he couldn't stand it anymore."

Trip to the vet? What vet?

People laugh at the rez dog. He's so pitiful. Worse than us. They laugh about their condition and how stupid they are. And the dogs, probably because of that defeatist mentality . . . and maybe hunger and the mange and ticks and general poor health . . . walk around like that. Like desper-ah-dos. You don't see them walking proud and bold and self-confident like those happy, off-the-rez dogs chasing Frisbees in the park.

Never laughing.

He's so pitiful. He's worse off than The People.

I don't think there's a Humane Society up here. If we had a Humane Society, they'd probably be more concerned about the owners.

After the Ceremony

You should have seen that old man holding that soup. After ceremony they asked him to pray, since he was the oldest there and a spiritual man. They fixed a "spirit plate," with a little pinch of everything they were having, and gave it to him.

It was a long time before he said anything at all, while all those assembled for the feast settled down to a few murmurs, then absolute silence. He was looking at the food, and there were tears in his eyes.

He began with an emotional appeal to the Creator and the Universe, coming to you as a poor, humble, common man, praying for his relatives. He thanked everybody. He prayed for everybody. He remembered everybody.

He thanked Grandmother Earth, and the Sky, and the Four Directions, and all the animals and plants and living things. He thanked the rain, and the Sun, and the wind. He thanked by name each of those plants and animals we were about to eat. He remembered everything. Everything.

The prayer grew long. People were looking up and glancing around. He prayed for the departed. He prayed for those in hospitals and jails. He prayed for the handicapped. He prayed for the homeless. He prayed for the hungry. He prayed for the leaders of the world . . .

Someone would say later, "AAAAIIIEEE . . . Long one. I was hungry, man. I was waiting for him to WRAP IT UP!"

He thanked the spirits, and the people who prepared the food and all their helpers, and all those people who helped bring that food to our table . . . "Thank you for everything, Tunkasila . . . Wo-pila . . . Mitakuye Oyasin."

Amen.

Everybody said, "Aho," and started getting in the serving line. Elders first, then the kids. Someone took the spirit plate outside.

Next ceremony, they asked that same old man to pray.

Uncle Joe Is Always Operating on Indian Time

Uncle Joe is always the last person to show up for sweat lodge. We stand around the fire, waiting and waiting for Joe to show up—you've got to wait, because he's a chief.

You wait for the chiefs, but they don't have to wait for you. You don't keep the chiefs waiting. You wait for them. So we'll stand around that fire, waiting for Joe. An hour or two earlier, someone would ask, "You call Joe?"

"Yeah. He said he'd be here."

Everyone looks back at the fire. We wait some more, each of us occasionally looking up over the hill toward the west for his headlights. Sometimes we'll proceed without him and Joe will show up just as we begin; but a lot of the time, we wait. "Let's go ahead and load the pipe, then," Tom usually says after waiting and waiting around the fire. "He's not gonna to show up until the rocks come in."

Maybe he comes late to make certain the rocks are hot. Maybe he's doing it to keep alive a cultural tradition.

It's simple. Joe operates on "Indian Time." It's a phenomenon in Indian Country. Indian Time means it's not going to happen until it's supposed to happen. Things don't start on time. It don't start until the people all get there. If they said "around dark," that could be anytime after dark, but not before.

Indian Time means late. Never early. Always late, and always a lot later than you expected. People laugh about it. "Runnin' on Indian Time" is being late.

It's not because Indians don't wear watches. And it's not because you can't find a clock on the wall in Indian Country. It's because in Indian Country time simply don't matter much. Nobody's in a hurry.

Nobody's in a hurry to do anything. The people here operate on a different time called waaaaay slowdown.

Visitors notice it. "Things are really slowed down around here," they'll say.

Gotta ratchet it back a few notches. In fact, sometimes time runs so slowly here you'd think you were moving backwards. Seems like that sometimes. The rest of the country is moving forward, and Indian people are moving backwards.

This is not to say that some of the people who work jobs don't have to attend to time, but even within the construct of a typical nine-to-five job, they're still functioning on Indian Time. They're running late. They're not where they said they'd be when they said they were supposed to be there. Like Uncle Joe.

"What time is it?" a visitor will ask. People look at them, then look up at the sun, then shrug their shoulders or maybe offer an approximation. At night they just ignore the question or look at you vacantly without answering. People can tell you what phase the moon is in, but they can't tell you the time.

Sometimes we lose track of days. "This is still Tuesday, innuh?" someone might ask.

"Nah. It's Friday."

"Geeeeeee. What month?"

Like Joe. We've been having sweat regular on Wednesdays and Sundays for three or four years, sometimes Fridays, too. Joe will call up on a Sunday and ask, "Is there sweat tonight?"

"Yeah. You coming?"

"Yeah," he says, "I'll be there. What time you going in?"

"Around sundown," we've learned to tell him if we don't light it until sunset, giving him two hours to get there, although he lives just fifteen minutes away. If we plan to go in later, we'll tell Joe, "Early. Right about sunset."

If we haven't lit the fire yet, we'll tell Joe it's been burning for two hours.

But then, Joe American Horse, who served twice as Tribal President and one term as tribal judge, still has his hands full for a guy who should be retired and has a right to be running on Indian Time. With Dottie away, Joe has to manage Timmy, his FAS (fetal alcohol syndrome) son whom they adopted as an infant and raised for the past fifteen years. As a teenager, Timmy, who drools, cannot feed himself or hold his head up, still wears diapers, and requires constant care, is nearly unmanageable at this age.

People say that Joe should put him in a home, but Joe can't do it. Even though Timmy can barely walk by himself, is unresponsive to communication, and cannot speak, Joe still cannot put him away somewhere. "I can still take care of him," he says.

But we wonder, is he trying to convince us, or himself? Maybe he can. But people say he's getting too old. Both Joe and Timmy. But Joe has time for Timmy, despite his driving elders to lunch, an active life, and showing late for sweat lodge twice a week. Joe has Indian Time for Timmy. That's why he's always late.

He brings him to lodge sometimes if he can't find a sitter. Timmy likes the fire. Seems to, anyway.

Sometimes Joe brings Timmy inside the lodge, and it seems like he really likes it. In there, we all ask the Creator to fix Timmy. We ask him to make it so Timmy could talk. One time, and it's the only time any of us had seen Joe weep, he asked for prayers to help Timmy.

But most of the time, Joe shows up by himself, or he'll leave Timmy in the car during ceremony.

Most of the time, he shows up late. Part of the reason is he's on Indian Time. But we've got to wait for him because he's a chief and he interprets for the Old Man, Ernest, who conducts our ceremonies and speaks only Lakota during lodge, the traditional way in which he was taught by his grandfather.

So Uncle Joe tells everyone the Old Man's opening remarks, then adds a few of his own in his meek, soft-spoken, humble way that is interspersed with moments of unintentional and spontaneous hilarity, like a few weeks back when he told a group of young volunteers, "This ceremony is ancient. It was here before Jesus. It was here long before the Caucasian race ever came to this planet."

Another time, he said, "We say 'Mitakuye Oyasin,' which means we are related to everything. We are related to the trees, the animals, the birds . . . the flies."

"Did Uncle tell those people we were related to the flies?" someone asked later, as everyone laughed.

He doesn't mean to be funny. He just is. He told another group, "Just pray like you're used to. You can pray to God in your own English."

Later, when people were laughing about it around the fire, Joe said sheepishly, "I meant to say 'language.'" If Yogi Berra has a counterpart in Indian Country, it would be Uncle Joe.

So, it's good when Joe is there at the beginning to interpret. Whenever he is finished speaking, he always says, "Thank you for your kind attention."

Uncle Joe teaches us humility. When he shakes your hand in greeting, he always looks at the ground.

And Joe, whose grandfather, Chief American Horse, was one of the treaty-signers, has traveled around the world making public speeches and is probably one of the most respected men on the reservation. He is recognized as a man with great integrity. An elder and a chief. It's therefore part of his responsibility to uphold and assure the cultural tradition of Indian Time.

That's why we wait for him.

Going After Commods

Drove into Pine Ridge Village today. It wasn't as depressing as the last time. There was a crew constructing a new bridge on the west end of town, and in the center of town, Big Bat's gas station, which was in the process of being rebuilt from the fire, was operating out of a large metal boxcar. Across the street, the tribe had recovered the tribal office buildings, which were commandeered by the Grassroots Oyate last year, and were restoring them. Things looked alive.

Took Lupe, my Mexican assistant, in to check his mail, and loaded my laundry, thinking to kill two birds with one stone. The other stone was our objective of "gaining" commods . . . the monthly government issue of black and white generic commodities that are high in sugar, fat, and carbs, and have left half the adult Lakota population with diabetes.

Why would anybody want them, you might wonder. They're free, is why.

Outside the long, low, red, concrete block building housing Sioux Nation, the major local shopping spot for groceries and the focal point of activity, traffic, and parking lot enterprises in the form of Indian tacos, drug sales, and an ongoing flea market, we avoided two drunks who knew us and whom we knew would try to hit us up for some cash.

"There's Kenny and Will over by the laundry mat," I said.

"They'll try to hit us up," said Lupe as we pulled into the parking lot.

We parked down on the other end of Sioux Nation, then drove slowly over to the laundry mat after they staggered past us, not recognizing my car.

There was a half-inch pool of water at one end of the laundry mat that we had to wade through to get in the door. Big signs in red block letters told us we could get tokens for the washers inside Sioux Nation. Had to use tokens. Don't need to ask. The collection boxes would be ripped apart if they used quarters.

A Vietnam vet named Mike came in with his old lady. Both of them were "tuned up," and wondering if we had five bucks for gas. They also knew where we could get a dime bag, Lupe said, and went off with them while I went for tokens.

Out in the car, while the wash was spinning, Lupe rolled up two "Pine Ridge pinners" (about the size of a lean toothpick) and gave one to Mike. We were preparing ourselves for the other one when another tuned up Vietnam vet approached the car, looking for some change.

I gave him what we had there on the console, and he proceeded to tell me his Vietnam experience, from the day he arrived "in country" to wherever it was I stopped him from telling any more. Should be about rinse cycle time.

Before we got out of there, a crusty older guy with red, watery eyes rolled his wheelchair over to the car and asked for a cigarette. Didn't ask for cash . . . just a smoke. Gave him two, and he wheeled away, saying "Pilamiya," thank you, with the lit cigarette dangling from his lips.

Got the laundry and headed out for the commod warehouse. Lupe insisted that we needed to go over to the welfare or food stamp office and get some paper-work before we drew commodities.

"You don't need to go through all that," I told him. "We can go directly to the warehouse."

"You gotta go to the food stamp place first," he said again.

"No you don't."

"Yes you do."

"No you don't."

"Yes you do."

"Hey Lupe," I said. "Just sit there and watch, okay? Watch closely. Just observe."

"Okay, okay," he said, sitting back in the seat with a heavy, disbelieving sigh as we pulled up to the warehouse.

"If I'm wrong, we'll go after the paperwork," I said. "I've done this before."

"Okay," he said, without saying, "we'll see," but I knew he was thinking it.

Breezed right through. Claimed commods for two—me and my son, who lives in Colorado but whom I expected to visit, so I needed the extra juice. The form requested where I lived, the number of people in my household, what income, if any, I have, and my signature underneath a statement saying that everything I wrote on there was truthful.

Signed it and gave it to Angie American Horse, a lady who looked really bored with her job inside that small office, separated by a lattice barricade from the front reception area.

From his raised-eyebrow expression, I could tell Lupe was surprised and impressed. Without telling me I was right, he immediately took a form from the wooden box on the table, filled out the paperwork, and followed me out the door and around the building to the side, where we waited inside a small, plywood cubicle that sheltered people from the elements while they waited in line.

A large sign inside the cubicle warned people with big, black Magic Marker letters, "IF YOUR DRINKING YOU WILL NOT BE SERVED," and to take everything you need, and "DON'T TAKE IT TO THE DUMP."

A Pepsi machine stood just inside the door, and behind it, a blue poster with a photograph of the Statue of Liberty on it read, "Land of the Free—Home of the Brave," proclaiming equal opportunity and nondiscrimination on the basis of race, religion, or gender. I guess Lupe and I qualified under those terms.

At "The Window," a smallish, narrow-faced, mixed-blood guy with a crew cut sat behind a computer terminal and hammered out a new entry. His nearly barren office held a file cabinet, multiple pictures of someone's kids tacked on the wall, and a large poster of a warrior with a pipe, praying to a huge white buffalo in the sky.

"Any turkeys?" I asked.

He looked up. "Huh?"

"Any turkeys?"

"No. Just chicken," he said, then asked me a series of questions as he typed my responses into the machine.

"Apples, oranges, or grapefruit? You can have two."

"Apples and oranges," I said quickly, like I'd done it before.

"Peanuts or peanut butter?"

"Peanut butter." The peanuts were horrible.

"Carrots, onions, or mixed vegetables? Pick two."

"Carrots and onions."

"Rice or spaghetti?"

"Spaghetti."

"Cornmeal, flour, or both?"

"Flour. Hold the cornmeal." The cornmeal was what you saw at the dump. That, and the prunes.

"Butter, oil, or shortening?"

"Butter."

"Pick two meats from the list," he said, looking up, catching my eye, and nodding at the list of 'Tuna, Chunky Stew, Lunchmeat, and Beef' in red Magic Marker that was taped on the wood, right there under my elbow.

"Tuna and chunky stew," I said. The lunchmeat, although preferred by nearly everybody I know, is a step down from Spam, if that's possible, looks and smells like dog food, and is a guaranteed sixteen-ounce can of cardiac arrest. But people like it.

"Okay," he said, ripping off the printout and handing it to me. "Wait till they call your name."

You could wait outside or inside, where you could sit on a long, blue bench. A half dozen guys worked by microwave headsets as the guy read through your list. Men in different areas pulled out the necessary items from skid loads of canned goods and smacked them down on a long, low counter that ran the length of the warehouse.

On the walls were pictures of smiling Smurfs carrying carrots, tomatoes, onions, and pumpkins. Upbeat, I guess. Everyone waiting there looked forlorn, like folks waiting for a bus or to be called in for their turn at the dentist.

When called, you got a long, flat, four-by-eight-foot, four-wheeled dolly to put your goods on and you went down the line and piled on your commodities. Just like Christmas, it sort of felt like. Most everyone was smiling as they left.

Outside, people loaded the goods from the cart to the trunks of their cars or the backs of pickup trucks. The lady next to us, who had jumper cables hanging out from under her hood, needed a jump, and the guy on the other side needed a push, since the starter was out on his truck.

A young guy pulled into the vacancy and we gave him our farina, since he has little kids, he said, who like it, and our potatoes, since we already had them growing in the garden. He didn't want the prunes.

In and out in less than a half hour. It pays to go later in the month, if you can wait that long and don't have a whole slew of kids, like the ladies who left there with their carts piled high and three or four young helpers to get it all loaded and home.

In addition to all the stuff they asked you to make a choice about, they gave you the regular stuff—potatoes, a package of stew fixings, cereal, Quaker Oats, canned fruit, canned veggies, canned juice, raisins, packaged pintos, packaged red beans, boxed macaroni, a couple of tubes of scary-looking, frozen, generic ground beef, and a couple packages of overmedicated, frozen, chicken parts. And prunes, just in case all the rest of that stuff didn't do the job.

Just Another Saturday
Night

I don't know how fast those two guys were going or who they were. They were drunk, is who they were. They were trying to outrun seven tribal police out here on Slim Buttes Road when they hit that big dip that I was telling you about and rolled their car.

They had three police cars from Oglala and four from Pine Ridge chasing them. Fortunately, they were drunk, and walked away from the wreck. Walked away from the wreck and into the hands of the police, who promptly arrested them. That was last night. Excitement in the neighborhood. A high-speed chase and rollover on Slim Buttes Road.

Then this afternoon, a longtime friend, Loren, his younger brother Ben, and their friend Moses, all came over here drunk, looking for wood for Camp Justice, where they've been keeping a fire going off and on since the murders of their brother, Wally, and Ron Hard Heart, over a year ago, just across the state line in White Clay, Nebraska.

Loren and Ben were staggering and reeking of alcohol, but coherent. Moses flopped heavily onto a metal folding chair and sat with his mouth open, staring at a spot in space about halfway across the room and about a foot off the floor. He didn't say a word during their entire visit.

I'd only seen Ben once since I saw him going down to the asphalt under the grip of a state cop when the vanguard of the most provocative of the post-murder protest marchers crossed the yellow tape the cops had stretched across the road. He gave me the tribal flag he was carrying and told me to take care of it as he was being hauled into the back of the paddy wagon. I gave the flag to a girl who was right there, and tossed Ben's hat to him.

Ben, along with Russell Means and four others, eventually were fined one hundred dollars each about a year later, and the entire chapter fizzled out of the limelight, except for Loren and a few others maintaining the fire at Camp Justice near the site on the rez side of the state line where the bodies were dumped. Those guys were sober for a long time after the murders.

"I don't have anything to trade," said Ben. "I've got a spare tire."

"You'd better keep your spare," I said. "I don't want your spare."

"I'll trade you HIM," Ben said, laughing and pointing at Moses, who laughed and sort of acknowledged the joke by raising and tilting his head slightly.

Loren just laughed. Ben went outside to his trunk and returned. "I've got this license plate," he said, handing me a dirty red 1986 tribal license plate that was made during the presidency of Joe American Horse as an expression of The People's desire to be recognized as a sovereign nation.

The plate was determined invalid in South Dakota by then-Governor Janklow, I think, but remains a popular collector's item on the rez, usually displayed on old cars from the outlying districts. Ben offered me the plate and a promised pack of smokes next time he comes out. Loren just laughed.

Despite the reservation being a welfare state, the sovereignty issue gets a lot of play in tribal council meetings and on KILI Radio, the tribal radio station. Along with some of the best programming in Indian Country, KILI routinely airs the monthly report from the Office of Public Safety, informing us of arrests, deaths by firearms, deaths by auto accidents, and other depressing statistics. The Office of Public Safety is otherwise known as the police force on Pine Ridge. The officers of the law here are the most polite and compassionate police I've ever seen. Here, where everyone knows or is related to everyone else, the police are often dealing with their relatives.

That day in White Clay when the murder protest mob of more than a thousand people pressed down upon the skirmish line of two dozen tribal police, the local officers stood dispassionate and self-composed as angry Indian protesters taunted and insulted them close enough to reveal the alcohol on their breath. Anywhere else in the country and there would have been some heads cracked open.

After a grocery store was looted and torched, and the fire truck that arrived to extinguish the blaze was commandeered and driven off, the public interest in a resolution of the yet unsolved murders waned. Daily life pressed back in upon The People and began to take its toll. Just Loren, it seems, and a few others have tried to maintain the cause and keep the fire burning at Camp Justice.

"That's a good trade," I told Ben, and shook the hand that had been permanently disfigured during an intoxicated weekend a couple of years ago. Ben and Moses filled the trunk of what could have been a yellow, 1984, low-riding Ford LTD, and the three men drove off lopsided, with the already busted rear springs sagging even lower.

So it's Saturday night and there's a party going on over at Bo's, according to Tom, who stopped there on his way back from Pine Ridge and found whatshisname from down there on "Gaza Strip" passed out on the floor.

Gaza Strip (the dirt cut-across from Slim Buttes Road to Pine Ridge) was named for the drinking that goes on down at "The Culvert," the swimming hole where the road crosses over the White River, and the occasional small arms fire, and notorious drinkers (not everybody, though) who live along it. The road is low, totally impassable following rain or snow, and traveled at one's own risk.

It's a dusty, deeply rutted, three-mile short cut, that can be traveled at seventy-five miles per hour in the turns when it's dry. Faster, with gunfire.

Actually, it's not that bad. I've never been shot at. But you do hear the gunfire. Who knows—it could be people hunting deer. Or it could be somebody busting caps at passing cars.

Actually, it's not that bad. It's not a hostile-fire zone. Just a free-fire zone.

So, to get over to Bo's to the party, you can take the Gaza Strip cut-across. Tom took it on the way back.

"That's nine in the community drinking," he said. "And one passed out."

Wally and Loren were stinking drunk that Saturday night four or five years ago when we headed from where I found them in Pine Ridge Village, out to Jun Little's in Oglala. All the way out there, sitting crammed right beside each other in the back seat, they kept saying over and over to each other, "I'mmmm gonna KICK yourrrrrr ass."

Then the other would say, "I'mmmmm gonna hit you so hard yourrrrrrr grandchildren are gonna feel it." And then they would both laugh, and they'd go through it again.

Another Sunday

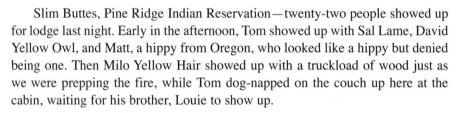

Slim Buttes, Pine Ridge Indian Reservation—twenty-two people showed up for lodge last night. Early in the afternoon, Tom showed up with Sal Lame, David Yellow Owl, and Matt, a hippy from Oregon, who looked like a hippy but denied being one. Then Milo Yellow Hair showed up with a truckload of wood just as we were prepping the fire, while Tom dog-napped on the couch up here at the cabin, waiting for his brother, Louie to show up.

We hadn't seen Louie for several months, but he stayed for a couple of hours, letting his van run with the lights on the whole time he was here. "I'm only going to be here a couple of minutes," he said.

Another pot of coffee, and Misty Sioux Davis called to say she was coming and bringing soup. "What time you going in?" she asked.

"Seven." A three-hour burn on the stones should be good.

More people showed up. Travis, a part-Cherokee and part-Lakota white guy and his wife, I guess, Lisa, came into the cabin and said they wanted to take in ceremony. She'd been in before, but it was a first for Travis. "If it gets hot, don't think about the heat—just focus on your prayer," they told him. Somewhere in there, Mark (won't say his last name) came over drunk and talking loud, apologized, then left after about an hour.

Aloysius Weasel Bear came up over the hill from his house down below. Stanley Blind Man came over, saying he needed a healing from the stabbing he'd received last week in Chadron at the hands of another Indian. Another pot of coffee, and Owen Warrior, one of the regulars, showed up, then Ben Good Buffalo.

Suddenly, everyone was out at the fire, leaving Louie up here at the house. We waited and waited for Uncle Joe, out of elder respect, and for Misty, who was bringing the soup. Finally, we went in. Right after all the rocks came in, Misty showed up on Indian Time with three of her five kids, along with Vickie Thunderhawk, Olowan and her boy, and another guy whose name I didn't get. "Make room for eight more," said Stan, who brought the stones. Everybody scooted over. Then, just before we began, Uncle Joe American Horse showed up and sat up front on top of the stone pit. A good seat. That was it. Three generations.

Lisa left right after the first round, and Travis departed after the second. After catching their breath, neither of them returned, but headed off home.

We told them earlier that it's good when children are in the lodge, because their energy is pure, and they show us adults how to sit. We're also encouraged by their interest in The Ways of their ancestors and to know the thread is unbroken.

Everyone got prayed for. God, Mother Earth, the spirit helpers, all living things, the departed, families of the departed, our leaders, our parents, our elders, our young people, orphans, the homeless, refugees, prisoners, those in uniform, vets, those who are suffering, Uncle Ernest, Tom's mashed toe, Milo's back, everyone sitting there, their families, Indians, you, everyone with whom we're connected, everyone who helps us, Running Strong, Onaway, Plenty, donors, volunteers, foreigners, everyone on the email list, nations, communities, families, marriages, Sun Dancers, vision questers, our enemies, and those who hate us. All our relations. Mitakuye Oyasin. Help, understanding, compassion, and all that. On the carrier wave of the songs, it got sent out to the Creator and the Universe.

Speaking in the packed lodge, Uncle Joe invited everyone to come anytime, Sundays or Wednesdays, telling them, "Sometimes there's only four of us in here . . . and I can lie down." (A typical, self-effacing comment—Joe never lies down.) Everybody laughed, and Owen said, "Sometimes we pray sideways."

In between rounds, someone asked about the two newcomers. "Where'd they go?"

"They went to eat soup," said someone in the dark, and everybody chuckled. Another voice repeated it, and everyone chuckled again.

Then someone added, "They're taking all the meat out of the soup," and everyone laughed out loud.

Afterward, twenty light-hearted people gathered in this tiny cabin with the four kids scampering right up into the loft, smiling down at the adults. Misty prepared a "spirit plate," in a small coffee cup, putting in a small portion of soup, a cracker, and a fragment of one of the biscuits I made that the boys thought were rocks. Tom made a prayer over the cup, and Misty sent it outside in the care of Kestrel. The lucky people got bowls, but the rest of us ate Misty's soup from coffee cups. It was loaded with meat. Everybody said, "Good soup, Misty."

The boys were talkative with anyone who would listen, having been accustomed to competing for air time among four siblings. Kestrel, who took in three of the four rounds, said that while we were singing during the last round, a little being with yellow eyes popped its head up behind the fire pit, then ducked back down again. "About this tall," he said, holding his arm out level with his chest. They say kids can see things us adults can't.

Kassel and his twelve-year-old sister, Krystal, who sat through all four doors, said they didn't lie down.

"I sat up the whole time," said nine-year-old Kassel, his face still flushed and red. "Me, too," said Krystal.

This morning, that spirit cup was empty.

The Old Man

That's what everybody calls him. Sometimes we call him Leksi (lek-shi), uncle. But everybody around the tiospaye and the ceremonies that he runs refers to him as "the Old Man."

Actually, he isn't that old. He's about . . . oh . . . .four years old, sometimes. But most of the time he's about twenty-five. During ceremony, he's about four or five hundred years old. Chronologically, he's seventy-seven, probably the youngest seventy-seven-year-old man on the reservation. Runs two miles every day, and attributes his good health to "this," he said one day, gesturing like he does, with both hands toward the sweat lodge.

Ernest is the eldest of seven brothers and has been the spiritual leader of the Afraid Of Bear tiospaye since the death of his brother Larue. In his introductory remarks as he began sweat lodge ceremony one day shortly after Larue's death, he told us, "When Larue was living, he sat here. Now it is my time to take care of this . . . for the next seven generations."

Ernest is the direct descendent of the brother of the famous medicine man George Sword, whose interviews, conducted by James Walker, constitute the bulk of *Lakota Belief and Ritual*, the bible of The Ways of The People. Ernest runs a twice-weekly sweat lodge here in Slim Buttes and presides over the Afraid Of Bear and American Horse Sun Dance, along with Vern and Joe American Horse, his first cousins.

Unassuming, humble, and sensitive, he's a sort of vaporous guy, doesn't let stuff stick to him, accepts things as they come, has a lively sense of humor, stays positive, and keeps his prayer in front of him.

That's pretty much his walk. After working with and around him for ten years, I believe his main lesson is humility.

"Awwwww, that's nothing," he said one day with a wave of his hand, putting some perspective on a rare but disturbing dispute I had with my sis. "Thaaat's nothing." He was right. We have a lot of work to do, and we all need each other.

He was married three times and has grown kids around. There are more adopted sons who call him "Ate" (Ah-tay, meaning "father") or "Tunkasi" (father-in-law), and even more people beyond the tiospaye who look to him for leadership. He never scolds, reprimands, or makes people uneasy.

"I didn't want to hurt their feelings," he'll often say, when holding back on something that maybe needed to be said. Weeks, maybe months later, he'll tell somebody else, knowing the word will get passed along circuitously to whomever it was intended. He'll never say something of a corrective nature directly to someone. I've never heard him say, "You should." He teaches in a grandfatherly way, and tells stories about the "early days," back when his grandfather was alive.

"Grandpa used to tell us a lot of things, but we were busy," he'll say, brushing his hands together like he was shooting out the door. "Geeeeeee, I wished I'd paid more attention."

Ernest loves to talk about his imaginary girlfriends, and, it seems, delights in getting on the nerves of his next-door neighbor, Bernice Brown Eyes.

"Hey. I'm gonna get married," he told her.

"Who?" she said. "What's her name?"

"I don't know."

"Well, what does she look like?" she said.

"Ahhhh. I don't know."

"How old is she?" she said.

"I don't know."

"Ohh, get on outta here."

He tells this story again and again. Then he'll just laugh and laugh, tickled by getting on Bernice's last nerve.

A confirmed bachelor ("I'm happy this way," he says), he's got "sixteen or seventeen" girlfriends and talks about some of the young ones. "I don't know what to think," he says. "She's pretty young."

"How old is she, Leksi?"

"Twenty-three, twenty-four."

"What's her name?"

"I don't know."

Ernest gets up every morning about five and prepares breakfast for his grand-children; he then drives them to two or three bus stops for school. When school's out each day, he goes back to pick them up. The whole flock of them.

Then he turns into a babysitter for his son and daughter-in-law, and a taxicab driver for whichever one of the kids needs to go somewhere, and from out here, it's usually Pine Ridge Village or Chadron, Nebraska.

On Wednesday and Sunday nights when he conducts sweat lodge, he tries to come over early. "I had to get the hell outta there," he says, escaping from babysitting duty. Sometimes he forgets his shorts and towel. "I had 'em laying right there when I left the house," he says. "And I went out the door and forgot them. Got to thinking about something else. Geeeeeee, I must be getting old."

Along with his sunglasses, he usually wears a baseball cap, blue jeans, old black shoes and a worn, light cotton shirt, pretty much the standard uniform of old men on the reservation. On the street, you'd never guess he was a spiritual leader. "A common man," an "ikce wicasa," is what he calls himself (the person he says we all should strive to be), although others might call him a holy man. He's definitely got the . . . authority. And he's got the power.

As an overseer at the Sun Dance, he runs sweat lodge once or twice a night for the people in the Main Camp, sometimes until 3:00 a.m. He has a sensitivity for first-timers and never has scalded anyone in ceremony, although people will exit shaking their heads at his power, endurance, and intensity.

"Geeeeee, it was hot," he'll sometimes say after ceremony, as if he had nothing to do with it.

Ernest and some of the other old guys love to tell stories about each other, usually on their escapades as young men, stretching the tale and adding an out-right lie or two or three, but still making it almost believable.

They like to hear me tell a fictional account of accidentally running into some of their offspring in Asia, where they served back during WWII. The story is told right there in front of them, telling the other old guys and everyone else standing around.

"What's your name?" I asked the kids.

"Afraid Of Bear," each of the eight young, half-Asian, half-Indian kids repeat, right down the line.

"Afraid Of Bear, Afraid Of Bear. Afraid Of Bear. Afraid Of Bear."

"Same mother?"

"Oh, no. No. Different muddah. Same faddah."

"My muddah, she say some day my faddah come back. Him NEBBA come back."

Those old guys get a good belly laugh and pick it up, telling it to each other again, changing the name, adding to it, twisting it, and making it funnier. They get to the end of the story and then just laugh and laugh and laugh.

They say back in the old days, before TV, that's what the people used to do for winter entertainment. They would get together and stand up and tell stories. Maybe a kernel of truth in there. Much of it stretched and distorted, but almost real enough to be believed. The winner for the night was the person who could be the most convincing and make everybody laugh.

Around the fire, Ernest will sometimes say something straight out of the blue, breaking what are often long silences as we wait to go into the sweat lodge.

"I just got out of the doghouse at twenty minutes after two, this afternoon."

"Out of the doghouse?"

"Yep. I had a shirt and a couple pairs of socks I had to get. I didn't want to go back. She said, 'Get the hell out,' and I told her, 'I heard you the first time.'"

We'll all laugh, and he'll repeat the final line of his fictional conversation, "I heard you the first time."

He'll go on, talking for both parties . . . "Well next ti . . . There WON'T BE NO NEXT TIME!"

You can tell he was married, just by the nature of his contentious conversation. After ceremony, when everybody is standing around joking and just sort of staring at the fire, the Old Man will finally announce, "Welllllll, I'd better be going, or I'll be in the doghouse."

Fact is, he's got to get home so he can get up and take the grandkids to the bus stop the next morning.

Everyone will laugh as he goes around the circle, shaking hands with each of us. Teasing him, someone might say, "She told him to come home right after it was over."

"Welllllllokay," he'll say, waving good-night to everyone. He's got some pet phrases he uses in response to just about anything. One of them is, "That's ohhh-kay. That's allllllllright."

Another is, "I didn't say anything."

Sitting here drinking coffee in the kitchen (he can drink a pot or two by himself), I asked him how long a person should prepare themselves to Sun Dance. He held up four fingers. "Four years," he said.

"Fouuuuuur years."

I nodded, and a silence fell over the kitchen.

"Or one," he added, holding up one finger. "Four years, or one year."

In that same conversation, raising an issue of concern among some of the more traditionally-minded people on the reservation, I asked him what he thought about all of the white people who are coming to the Dance. Again, he held up four fingers.

"There's four colors," he said. "Red, White, Black, and Yellow. Anybody who wants to pray with us can come pray."

His brother, Larue, once said in sweat lodge over in the canyon as we prepared for the first year of the Dance to be held there on the grounds of the Wild Horse Sanctuary, "There will be people come from the four directions. Don't turn anybody away."

Whereas Larue was more remote and quiet, with a limited use of English, Ernest is outgoing and funny.

Utterly hilarious at times. But when he goes into the lodge, he morphs into a different person. "Laying down" the white language and using only his native Lakota during ceremony, he speaks through an interpreter and is all business. Only afterwards, back around the fire after ceremony, does he return to his comical self.

"My grandpa told us when we go in there we should lay down all our laughing and joking around. Then when we come out, we can pick it up again." Ernest has told me this message from his grandfather about a dozen times and repeated it to others. "But while we're in there," he says, "we should just be praying. Praying to God."

So if anyone is wondering how they should behave in the sweat lodge, they can observe the Old Man. He stays focused on his prayer, and when the door is open and the water is being passed around, he stays quiet, doesn't ever laugh at anything being said; and when the water dipper comes around to him, he continues his prayer with the water.

I've never, ever seen Ernest lie down in the lodge. Never. He always sits up like a stone Buddha, despite the heat and intensity that drive younger men to the ground and sometimes drive people out the door.

When we have visitors, including elderly white people, touring the reservation who express apprehension of going into the sweat lodge, Tom, his son-in-law, will tell them, "No problem. No problem. The man who runs it is seventy-seven years old."

They're relieved . . . until we get in there and the Old Man turns up the heat and drives their faces into the dirt. Yep. He can make you get close to Mother Earth. When he knocks us down on a particularly hot lodge, we sometimes come out and ask each other, "Do I have mud on my lips?"

I've never seen him angry, nor have I ever seen him take offense at anything anybody said. The closest harsh thing I've ever heard him say about anyone was in reference to the younger, "overnight medicine men," when he once delivered a line that us younger guys picked up on. "That guy over there . . . he knows a little something . . . but that other guy over there . . . he knows it allllll."

Unlike Beatrice, the matriarch of the tiospaye, whose influence is reservation-wide, Ernest, as the spiritual elder of the family, is more concerned with the local matters of the extended family, although through the Sun Dance he has many off-reservation contacts across the country.

He likes to tell about his trips to the VA hospital for routine physical exams. Each time, he checks what he thinks might be wrong with him . . . his heart, his blood pressure, and so forth, in hopes of drawing a disability pension. After the exams, the doctor tells him, "Well, there's nothing wrong with you, Mr. Afraid Of Bear. You can go back to work now, or whatever you were doing."

About The Ways

Had a house full of people again today. Lupe arrived back on the scene as mysteriously as he disappeared. Down in Scottsbluff and up in Rapid, he said. We got a load of wood and then met back up here, where Lupe made some bean and cheese burritos. Tom came up from base camp, the Old Man stopped by, and some other Sun Dancers came through.

Ernest left shortly after a cup of coffee, telling everyone he'd see us tomorrow night at sweat lodge. He had to get right back or he'd be "in the doghouse," as he says.

While sitting around the table and drinking coffee, talk led to the Sun Dance, now only four and a half months away. A number of things were discussed, including the presumptuousness of some people who circumvented the protocols of the invitation process and thought they could just show up and start dancing, without speaking to the sponsor (Tom), or the lead dancer (also Tom).

While the discussion shifted to the preparation, the same sentiments were aired. One of the dancers remarked about his eleven years of preparing before entering the arbor, and now, "after three sweat lodges, they think they're ready to dance," he said.

Lupe spoke about how one should approach the Sun Dance leaders or elders and give them tobacco first, before asking their advice concerning either The Ways, or desire to be involved in the Dance.

"Overnight Indians," said another of the men seated around the table. "Everybody wants it to happen right now, and they don't know how to go about it. They think they're ready, but they're not."

"I told those people, 'Hey, time out. Before you go waltzing in there thinking you're going to dance, you need to check with the sponsors first. The men need to talk to Tom; he's the Sun Dance leader. And the women need to talk to his wife, Loretta. They're the leaders and the sponsors.'"

Maybe it's the planetary alignment. Maybe it's the Age of Aquarius. Maybe it don't take as long as it used to. Maybe there's a sense of urgency now.

Some of the dancers (one of whom took fifteen years before dancing), voice similar disdain for those who prematurely jump in, for reasons known only to them.

"I think they're missing the whole point," said one of the men. "It's not something you rush into. There's a reason it takes years to get yourself ready to step in there. You have to be really certain about what you're doing in there."

It's true. At this Dance we've seen more than one person come and dance one year, never to return. "Those people don't understand," said Loretta, one day in her kitchen. "They don't know what commitment means, and their lives are gonna be like that. They didn't know how hard it was going to be."

A few years ago, one young man decided on the morning of the fourth day that he wanted to dance. He said he was going to pierce in the morning and pull skulls in the afternoon. A couple of the dancers stopped him, knowing better, but they let him dance, and by God, they let him pierce! He passed out shortly thereafter, and we propped him up against the tree. When he regained consciousness, they made him go back to his spot and continue dancing. He never returned the following year.

"That kid had no more business in that arbor than the man in the moon," said one of the veteran dancers at the time.

Some of the women who danced never came back, finding more important things to occupy their lives than to attend the Dance again. Some men, too.

"There's only two reasons you should miss the Dance," a dancer once said. "Either someone in your family dies, or you die."

"You know, it's a four-year commitment," a prospective dancer was told.

It's scary, that commitment. It's a big step. It's not something one does to say you've done this in your life. It's something that changes your life.

Trapjaw

"Trapjaw," Henry Red Cloud exclaimed over the phone. "He's got trapjaw. My uncle had one like that that got his mouth caught in a trap, going after meat," he said.

I don't know. It seemed like there would have been demonstrations of other marks on his muzzle if he'd been stuck in a trap. But as it was, the only thing left of his lower jaw was one of the lower incisors and some bone and a few front teeth. What was there was hanging by the skin of his lower lip. It was beginning to putrefy.

"I suppose you saw stuff like this all the time in Vietnam," said Tom, shaking his head and coming back in the house from the deck. "Bone and gristle and . . . "

"Exposed tissue . . ." I said. "Yeah."

"I don't know why somebody would do something like that," said Bo Davis, walking in circles in the kitchen and cutting his eyes at the dog like he really didn't want to look at it. "You'd have to be sick." Bo was convinced he'd been shot. Sal, too.

Sal Lame sat quietly on a stool, drinking coffee and looking mostly at the floor. "He's not gonna recover from this one, I don't think," I said to Sal, up close. Sal glanced up at me and shook his head.

Misty Sioux Davis, who for some reason, was riding along with the guys in the pickup, sat at the table with a Pepsi and the phone. "That's Marvin's dog, inna?" she asked. "He's got a gun."

"Marvin said it wasn't his," I said. "But he came from over that way because his girlfriend lives over there . . . I've got a gun, right here." Misty called up Marvin next door and relayed the story through a third party, but I can't tell you exactly what she said, because I wasn't paying attention. Too many people were talking at once. Ended with something to the effect of, "tell your dad to bring his gun."

Those guys had already been through here earlier in the day and had gone down over the hill to the base farm, spinning and fishtailing up and over the hill in the ruts of a foot of snow that was beginning to melt and turn the ground to soup. Three or four of us had already been mired stuck since the snow fell last week. Days like this on the reservation, a lot of people stay home.

"We don't have to do anything, RIGHT NOW," I said before they left. "Let's give him another day in the sun."

"Yeah," said Bo. Another day in the sun . . . sundown."

I don't know who adopted whom. A lot of dogs come through here looking for handouts, just checking.

Mr. Fuzz, who looked to be a collie-shepherd mix, came over one day and allowed me to remove the burrs out of his long fur. Then, after seeing he could be here on a fairly regular feeding schedule, kept coming back until he finally decided one day to stay. Been here ever since.

My car was stuck between here and the road, over by Rex's, a half mile from the house, and when I trudged back here with Frankenstein feet in boot-sucking gumbo, I found Fuzz lying there on his bed of straw under the bird feeder, blood all over chest and paws, his lower jaw hanging down and mostly gone. He had been gone the entirety of the previous day.

"THERE you ar . . . . Whaaaaaaaaat happened to YOU?" I asked him, stunned.

He glanced up at me sheepishly, then looked down, then back up. Then back down. He was really hurt, he said. Really hurt.

I stroked his head and got down close to examine the wound. He didn't want to lift his head. Looked like he'd been shot. Blown away. I'd seen that sort of wound before. Looked like he'd eaten his last meal.

I put some water down, but he couldn't even lap it up. Part of his tongue was gone, too.

But from the top, looking down at him, you really couldn't tell he was hurt, except for all the blood. His face and his muzzle were intact and looked fine. He had that same expression and look, looking down on him.

Didn't know exactly what to do. Call a vet? Rez dogs don't see vets. Ever in their life. They depend entirely upon the Creator. They're either gonna make it, or they're not.

"That's the same guy who took a round up the ass last fall," I said to Tom, as he stood there in the doorway looking at Fuzz lying in the sun on the deck. "He fully recovered after lying around for a week or so, and then a couple of months later, he raced me out to the sweat lodge, running full tilt and just LEAPING through the grass, looking back at me over his shoulder with his tongue lolling out, just to show me."

Bo just kept walking around in the kitchen, smoking a cigarette and shaking his head. "I can't BELIEVE someone would do that to a dog," he kept saying, "and leave him like that."

"Must've run off after he was hit," said Sal.

I put out some chili, cheese, and crackers, and fixed another pot of coffee. Bo set up the chessboard, and Misty checked her email. Sal sat quietly and Tom kept going in and out the door, looking over Mr. Fuzz.

"He can't eat," he said. "He can't even get a drink."

"Yep. But look at him. He's up and around. He acts like he wants to live."

"He's just gonna fade," said Misty. "You oughta just shoot him."

Yeah, well. We all knew that. That's what Ruben Quinn, the white rancher who grazes his cattle on local land leases said when he called back to tell me his wife was a PhD nutritionist, not a vet. He told me, after listening to my phone message, that he occasionally has to put one of his cows down, and how he hates to do it, but he puts his mind on something else, and just does it.

"Lethal injection?" I asked him.

"No," he said. "I shoot 'em."

While Tom talked to Ruben about another matter, Sal and I walked out onto the deck. I sat down by Fuzz and stroked his neck, scratched him behind the ears, and talked to him. He had fleas.

Just around sundown, Tom placed his hand on my shoulder, and asked, "Well, Bro. Where's your gun? If you don't want to do it, I will."

"I've never killed anything, man," I told him. "I was a medic. I think I got that hunter-killer thing out of me in a former lifetime . . . 'cept flies. I hate flies."

Tom, a former 25-year ironworker in the tradition of Mohawk men, wanted to give him "The Mohawk Chop," he said, to the back of the head, making a sharp cutting motion with his hand. "We know how, now," he said, drawing closer, as if to tell me a secret.

"Mohawks've got the chop."

"Naw, man. I've got a gun," I told him, and gave him the .22 rifle and the clip from on top of the refrigerator. We walked outside and he slapped in the clip, locked and loaded.

Fuzz got up and walked off the deck, looking not at me, but at Tom. He knew. He walked away from us, slowly, like he was walking on eggs, not taking his eyes off of Tom.

"He knows, man. He knows," I said. Tom moved toward him, and Fuzz moved away.

"Nope. Nope. He knows," I told Tom, and stopped him. I took the rifle from him. "Sorry, man. Thanks, but . . . let's give him another night. Give him another night. Maybe he'll wander off somewhere . . . you know."

"Yeah," said Bo. "Dogs'll do that. They'll go off somewhere and die."

"Okay, Bro," said Tom. "It's up to you."

JEEsus, what a relief. I removed the clip, ejected the live round, fired the empty rifle, opened the bolt back up and came inside the house. All four of those guys piled into Dorf and spun off through the mud toward the highway. Fuzz came back up on the deck and stretched out.

I put him in the field, laid out some tobacco, and said a prayer for the good entry of his spirit into the dog spirit world after my neighbor Marvin came over and shot him at dusk while I was inside helping his grandson up the stairs to the loft, which all the little kids want to do when they come in here. The sound of the rifle kind of caught me by surprise.

Double Row
on a Wednesday Night

It was windy again. Too windy to plant carrots. The wind blew steady all day at about thirty to forty miles per hour, with gusts up to sixty. Irritating to stay out there too long. Yesterday and the day before were the same.

Unrelenting wind. A week of it. The water blew sideways out of the pump.

Everything not nailed down got blown away, and some things that were nailed down got blown apart. And after the wind blew first from the north, then the south and east before returning to the prevailing west, all the paper, plastic, and trash that had blown away was back where it started.

People began showing up early for sweat lodge, with the door either flying open or slamming closed as they entered the house. Tom Cook, Manuel Martin, and Lupe came up for morning coffee from down over the hill where they were working in the greenhouse, planting seedlings that would later be distributed across the reservation to those participating in Tom's gardening program, the main economic engine here, funded primarily by Running Strong for American Indian Youth.

Then Bo Davis stopped up for coffee and a game of chess. He too, was working on finishing up one of the two new greenhouses that had been framed last summer by the Foxmaple timber frame people from Maine. In between moves and fifty-mile-per-hour wind gusts, I picked up blowing trash and rebuilt my arbor that had been blown apart last week.

The crew left, and returned again around noon for bean, cheese, tomato, onion, and avocado burritos, and commodity macaroni and cheese. Watecha, who used to be Sandy's dog but has been hanging around for a month or so, chased the trucks down over the hill and later chased them back, awaiting Fuzz's daily ration, since Fuzz took a bullet to the back of the head and can no longer eat nor guard the place.

Those guys went back to work, then showed up a couple of hours later.

"It's too windy to work," they said. Better to stay up here, drink coffee, thumb through literature, and listen to the BBC.

About 3:00 p.m. the Old Man showed up on foot.

"How'd you get here?" asked Tom.

"I walked," he said. "Ran out of gas."

"Walked?" It was about three miles, by the way the crow flies, from his house to here.

"How'd you get across the river?"

The Old Man made a walking motion with his fingers.

"You walked on water?"

"Waded across," he said. "Took off my shoes and socks and pants and tossed them to the other side.

"It's about this deep," he said, holding his hand palm down, level with his chest. "Used to do it all the time."

"Eeeeeeeeeeyaaaa. Wasn't it cold?"

"Yep," he said. "That water's stillllllllll cold. That sweat lodge is going to feel good tonight."

At about 4:00 p.m. the guys began showing up, heading straight out to the lodge. Owen Warrior, Big Mike,

Ron Holton, and another guy, a first-timer, went out and stripped down the lodge, already partially disassembled by the wind.

They began the twice-weekly ritual of prepping the lodge for ceremony, cleaning the fire pit and rock pit, pulling the mats, stacking the fire, and chopping wood.

Then Uncle Solomon Red Bear, from way out on the other end of the reservation at Potato Creek, showed up with his wife, Rachael, and their daughter. Leaving the women in the car, Solomon came in the house with his pants hanging low on his ass, Lakota-style, finished the last burrito, and sat on a stool smoking a cigarette with a quaking hand, the ash dropping onto the floor.

After the fire had been going an hour or so, old Uncle Ike Yellow Bull showed up, shortly before four or five of the Red Cloud boys. Then Lupe's son, Chachee, showed up with his wife and little girl. A bit later, Misty Sioux Davis showed up with her two daughters, her sister, and her friend Vickie, followed by a couple of other Lakota women whom I didn't know, but they wanted to sweat here because it was safe, and they wanted to avoid the harassment they were getting where they had been going, they said.

There were people from Porcupine, Wounded Knee, Pine Ridge Village, and Potato Creek, along with the core group of locals. Soon everyone was gathered around the fire, waiting for Joe American Horse, who'd just returned from Germany.

"How many rocks?" asked Uncle Solomon.

"All of 'em, plus two."

Avery Red Cloud pulled out a water drum, and Tom sang four peyote songs at the fire as the Old Man stood smoking a cigarette and looking off to the west for Uncle Joe's car. Here he came.

"Get ready. The Old Man's going in."

Everyone scurried to their cars. Soon there was a long line behind the four uncles, and we respectfully waited for them to enter first. Then everyone else filed in behind them.

"Won't be able to lay down tonight," people said, teasing each other about having to sit up.

Twenty-four went in, making it a packed house, and unusual for a Wednesday night.

"Pack it in. Four more." People kept coming. "Make two rows."

People were practically sitting on top of the rock pit. All the rocks came in glowing red. After the first door, six people went out to catch their breath. Two of them didn't return. After the second door, the little girls and another half-dozen people departed, glistening with sweat in the light of the fire, some of them flopping down on pieces of carpet, steam rolling off their bodies.

Someone out there exclaimed, "Jesus!"

The Old Man was driving them out. Uncle Solomon went out. Some sat out a door, then came back. Everybody else was panting and grateful for the dipper of water when it came around. Some were sprawled out flat on their backs, finding room to lie down when people left.

Twenty-two people exited the lodge at the end, like the cartoons of a multitude of Indians pouring out of a tiny tipi. People dried off and got dressed, shook hands with each other, and stood around the glowing coals of the fire pit under an almost full moon. Jupiter, Venus, Mercury, and Mars shone brightly in the western sky. You could hear the water running in the White River, down over the hill. The coyotes were quiet. The wind had stopped.

Larue's
Hanblecheya Song

It's interesting at times to hear Lakotas, usually the elders, speak of the past in present tense. They make something that happened years ago sound as if it happened just today. The deceased are spoken of as if they're still here.

"Steven knows all the songs," the Old Man said of his brother Steven, the singer among the brothers, who died a decade ago.

The Old Man had songs on his mind.

"I got that song," was the first thing he said when he came in and sat down. We knew what he was talking about without any further reference.

The song came to him in the middle of his prayer, he said, one night in lodge about a month or so ago.

"And then . . . I couldn't remember it," he said. "I was right in the middle of my prayer," he explained, almost apologetically, "and I could hear Larue singing in my ear. Then . . . it's gone," he said, throwing up his hands helplessly and then staring sort of dejectedly at the floor, lost in thought.

He told this same story about twice a week for the past month. "Just couldn't grab it," he said.

Then today, before he waded across the river to get here, he stopped at his brother Richard's place.

"I went over to Richard's and asked him to sing his songs, seeing if he could remember it," Ernest said.

"He sang his songs, but nah . . . ," he said, shaking his head.

"Then when I got down to the river, I sat down to take a break and have a cigarette, and . . . it came back to me," he said, again throwing his hands out quickly, like he was catching a basketball.

"Let's record it," said Tom, knowing that was the only way we'd be able to catch it and also keep it, just in case it slipped away from Ernest again. He finished his cigarette and cup of coffee, then picked up the drum. Lupe leaned across the table, listening intently as the Old Man sang through one verse.

We thought we'd gotten all the old songs they could remember. The last we'd gotten was an old pipe-loading song from Larue, shortly before he died after the second year Sun Dance in the canyon. But here, two years later, the Old Man came up with another one.

"There it is," he said when he finished. "That's it."

"That's Larue's song," he said. "He uses it on hanblecheya."

Your Better Mind

Just when everybody was saying, "It looks like we ain't gonna get no winter this year," here up and comes a bigass snowstorm that nobody predicted. Nailed us blindside as a sucker punch. Never saw it coming.

Went into ceremony Wednesday night with just a dusting on the ground, and came out two hours later looking at a half foot of snow. And just an hour ago, we were in there thanking the Wakinyan (Thunderbeings) for bringing Mother Earth the moisture she so desperately needed.

Ten inches before it was done. Maybe a foot. More in some places. Snowed all day Thursday. Took 'em until 3:00 p.m. today (Friday) to get a plow out here on Slim Buttes Road.

"We could've been neighborhood heroes today if we had that road grader going," said Tom, here in the kitchen as we informed Big Mikey, who was sitting here drinking coffee with a puddle collecting at his feet, that TODAY is the day that tow truck drivers make their money.

Told him, "Man came on the radio talking 'bout, 'If you ain't behind the wheel of a tow truck, a road plow, a poe-leese car, or an ambulamps, then STAY HOME.'"

"Man on the TV set said, 'If you don't absolutely have to go nowhere, like the hospital, then STAY HOME.'"

"And you thought, 'They must be talking to everyone else in South Dakota but ME.'"

So there he went, headed into Chadron in a blizzard. Got turned sideways just this side of the line, down by the Slim Buttes Trading Post, and here, the next thing he knew, he was in the ditch. Wasn't too bad at first, he said, until he tried to get out. Then, being a man, he tried to get unstuck from the predicament he found hisself in.

Got in further.

Me myself, my better mind told me, "Keep your ass right at home and keep that fire going. Don't go nowhere."

And so this time I listened. This time I listened to my better mind, like I should have two weeks ago when I came down with a ten-day, heaping, Wakinyan cold after going out in subzero temps with a twenty-five-below wind-chill to take the half-ton Dorf into town.

"There isn't any gas in it," I told Tom. "She's sitting on empty. Won't make it."

"Yes it will," he said.

"No it won't," I said.

"Yes it will," he said. "There's a quarter tank."

"I just looked," I said. "It's empty."

"You can make it," he said. "The gas gauge is off a quarter tank."

I knew better. We . . . Lupe was with me . . . ran out of gas just about a mile or so outside of town.

Nothing out there to stop that arctic hawk from coming down from Canada, sweeping across the Tetons, gaining strength in the Black Hills, and blasting into my right ear drum.

So this time, I listened to my better mind.

"I should've listened to my better mind," said Tom, shaking his head and trying to thaw out here by the stove after pulling Big Mikey out of the ditch. "Now I've got a truck with a blown engine. I should've just stayed home."

Probably. But he couldn't. He had to come and pull Mikey out of the ditch and take Bo Davis and his daughter, Krystal, home. Bo and Krystal were here all day after they brought the two-ton dump truck, La Roja, back and got her stuck out in the field trying to make it back out to the road.

"Why didn't you go out the same way you came in, instead of heading out across country?" I asked him, when they came back to the house, dejected. I fixed more coffee, a pizza, and set Krystal up on the Internet while Bo and I set up the chessboard, waiting for Tom to come out from town.

"I was afraid I'd get high-centered," Bo said. "The drifts in the driveway are too high."

The drifts weren't the only thing that was too high. They got stuck out there after giving up on Tom making it out from town. Shortly thereafter, Tom showed up with Big Mikey in the '71 Ford four-wheel drive.

"See what impatience will get you?" said Bo. "I should've listened to my better mind. I should've just sat right here and waited."

After three or four pots of coffee and thawing out, all four of them headed out. They got as far as the truck cab, then came back inside. Truck wouldn't start.

"Won't fire," they said. "No fire."

Pulled out the battery charger and gave the battery a boost while Bo got under the hood and wired the choke partially open, since the carburetor linkage was messed up, Tom said.

"Heee's going to feeks it," he said, warming his hands on the stove before kicking off his boots and laying down on the couch. Mike sat drinking coffee and making a new puddle under the kitchen table, and Krystal played outside in the snow with the dogs before coming in and shivering in front of the stove.

And since the best mechanics in the country are on reservations, and since Bo is one of the best mechanics around, by God, he fixed it with baling wire and a pair of needle-nose pliers. After the boost, she started right up, and everybody headed out. A couple hours later, Big Mikey and Tom returned in Big Mikey's truck. He was all happy now, since his truck was out of the ditch. But Tom was bummed out, since in the process he blew his engine.

Mike headed off over the hill, and Tom crawled up into the loft after phoning Loretta and eating peanut butter and crackers. The dogs crawled between the straw bales under the bird feeder. Sometime during the night it stopped snowing.

Then today . . . hey . . . it's a new day! Sun was out, snow was melting, dogs were happy to be alive . . . a beautiful, snow-packed day in Indian Country.

Big Mikey showed up to take Tom home and finished off the fried potatoes and eggs before I gave them to the dogs. Started shoveling out and got La Roja unstuck, then made a half dozen passes up to the road and back in La Roja, blazing a trail for the dozen or so dancers who'll be coming in here tomorrow for a tune-up dancer's lodge in prep for the Sun Dance, now a mere three months away.

About the third day of the Dance, I thought today while clearing a path to the woodpile, I'm gonna remember how good this cold snow feels on my bare hands.

Around the third pass down the driveway, I got La Roja stuck when I drifted too far to the right, out of the tire ruts. Lucky for me, Big Mikey was just returning from town and backed his four-wheel-drive pickup back to the big red dump truck.

Using a tire between two chains for a bungee effect, he surged forward and snapped one of the chains, one end slapping back into his rear window, and the other snapping back into La Roja's windshield.

"Cheap shit," he said, holding up the end of the chain. "We're lucky we didn't break our windshields," he said, refastening the one good chain directly to the bumpers.

"Yeah. Take it easy this time," I replied, getting back into La Roja.

Big Mikey took off again with all four wheels spinning and spitting snow, apparently unconcerned about the two feet of slack in the chain.

WHANNNGGGG. He yanked me forward as his wheels spun, and out she came, grudgingly. Mike pulled me forward thirty yards before coming to a dead stop. I forgot that La Roja had no brakes, and the pedal went to the floor.

I waved frantically at Big Mikey, trying to motion him to move forward, but he was already getting out when La Roja slammed into his rear bumper. WHANNNGGGGG.

From a distance, we must've looked amusing, checking for damage out there in the snow.

"Didn't hurt mine none," said Mike. "That was already there when I bought it," he said, pointing at the dent in his bumper. No problem either, with La Roja's armor plate.

Mike took off for Rapid City, and I made another pass on the driveway before sundown, mashing down the snow between the ruts with La Roja's dual rear tires, so those boys coming out tomorrow in their low-rider city cars won't get stuck.

"You can always drive Dorf," I said to Tom.

"No four-wheel drive," he said. "She won't make it."

"Yes she will," I replied. "Dorf don't get stuck. It's the gas gauge that's stuck."

Sun Dance Fever

Everybody chuckled sort of nervously when one of our overseeing elders, Dave American Horse, told the assembled men in the men dancers' sweat lodge the morning of the first day, "You don't ever quit Sun Dancing."

As the person who conducted, or "ran" the lodge, Dave sat in the eleven-o'clock position, relative to the door. He said he'd been at it for something like twenty-seven years, I think, and told us, "You just can't quit. It's a way of life."

And it's a way of life for thousands of Lakotas in this season of Sun Dancing, roughly June though August.

The season of Sun Dancing and vision questing. It's hot. Really hot. A suffocating Moab, dry-wind hot. We're glad, in these days of temperatures topping out at a blistering 115 degrees in the shade, that we finished our Dance in the canyon by mid-June solstice when our worst day was only 103.

It's hard to describe the Sun Dance to someone who has never attended one, and sometimes up here in Indian Country where the Dance is the center of Indian lives, prayers, and culture, we lose sight of the fact that what we practice is an extreme and marginal form of worship about which most of America hasn't the vaguest idea. "Sun Dance?" they sometimes ask. "Can you show me a few steps?"

One could talk about the color, and the pageantry, and the power of the songs and drum. One could describe the choreography and the magical, spiritual high of the Dance. You could talk about the sacred tree and the beauty of all the prayer ties and flags that adorn it. One could relate the incredible, heart-wrenching, individual sacrifices being offered within the arbor. But still, without being there, it would be difficult to capture the power and the entirety of the event.

The four-day Sun Dance is the most sacred and central of the seven sacred rites of the Oglala Lakota.

Comparatively speaking, it is Thanksgiving, Christmas, and Easter all rolled into one. It is the time of year when all the relatives gather to celebrate life and offer up sacrifices of one form or another. People will fast and go without water for four days, pull skulls, hang from the tree, or simply dance under the blazing sun.

People in attendance can go to support the Dance in various forms. Work around camp, cut wood, work in the kitchen, help out, or show direct support to the dancers and the singers by being present under the arbor.

Of the estimated fifty-plus Sun Dances held annually across the reservation, people around here will generally ask, "Where?" "How many dancers?" or, "Who's running it?"

Some of the more renowned Dances attract hundreds of dancers from around the world, drawing yellow, black, and white people, as well as red.

"So and so's having a Dance over near Porcupine," they'll say. "Over a hundred dancers."

— — — — —

The Lakota claim ownership of the Sun Dance, although other tribes across the North American continent are said to have practiced it. The Lakota say it was theirs, and perhaps rightly so, for here, the language and ceremonies and customs remained intact when others were snuffed out and paved over by American culture.

Here, it was never lost. The Dance went underground with the traditional ways and the Native American Church from 1882 to 1934, when the non-Indian culture-at-large was at its most repressive, trying to stamp out the language, the religion, and the influence of the medicine men, and replace the buffalo with a gardening hoe.

Perhaps that's why some traditionally-minded people wish to restrict the religious ways of the people to Indians only. "Whites have taken everything," they'll say. "And now they want to take our religion."

Such views are understandable, given the nation's history. Those holding this perspective believe they are protecting The People and view themselves as guardians of the culture by keeping it pure. They claim the pipe was given to the red man, which no one seems to dispute. "We don't want to see it get watered down," said an Oglala friend.

Beyond that, others will openly invite anyone to participate and pray with us. "I see white brothers and sisters out there shedding their flesh and blood," said Milo Yellow Hair one day during a discussion on the topic of white participation. "Inside that arbor, the Creator doesn't recognize color."

That's comforting to many whites who take part in Indian ceremonies, and to those who conduct ceremonies inclusive of whites, but others see the sweat lodge and the Sun Dance as exclusively Indian and forbid white participation. Others even wish to prevent other tribes from performing the Dance, including Hopis and Navajos. "They never did have the Dance until the Lakota brought it to them," said one Indian writer in an opinion article.

Nevertheless, one will see Lakota songs and ceremonies practiced by Indians across the country. One can find Lakotas conducting ceremonies in nearly every major U.S. city, and in foreign countries, particularly European.

So, there's also controversy surrounding the Dance, despite its being sacred and holy. Just last week, they say a Dance over at Porcupine got busted by the BIA (federal Bureau of Indian Affairs) cops for whites dancing with eagle feathers, a no-no among the feds and many Indians.

And in our own Dance over in the canyon, off the reservation, there's about a fifty-fifty mix of Indians and whites. The people got along fine, and there was a positive atmosphere of spiritual brotherhood and sisterhood throughout the four days. Everyone abided in their higher self.

When we returned home to the reservation, exhausted and dehydrated from the four-day ordeal, we relaxed on the deck and entertained guests who had traveled across the country to attend or participate in the Dance. We were finished, for another year. At a thank-you sweat lodge shortly after our return, someone said, "We've only got 361 days till next Dance. Better start getting ready."

And floating up the river was the sound of a drum. It was 109 degrees. Our neighbors to the north, a few miles away, were on their fourth day, about to wrap it up.

Up in Porcupine, over in Allen, up at Wounded Knee, and over in the badlands at "The Fortress," they were about to begin.

Counting to Seven

A couple summers ago, when the high school volunteers in camp were preparing to go into the sweat lodge, one of the young men with whom I'd been working the fire requested at the last minute to be the guy who carries the stones.

What that is, is bringing the stones on a pitchfork from the fire pit to the lodge, once all the people are in there and ready. "Sure," I said. "You bring 'em, I'll catch them."

He was really nervous and wanted to do everything right. "Don't worry about it," I told him. "But if you drop one, take it back to the fire and bring it last."

He repeated the procedure. "First the cedar, then the antlers, then the pipe, then the first seven rocks, right?"

"Right," I told him. "Then the pipe comes out, then bring the rest of the rocks. Someplace else, they might do it different, but here, that's the Old Man's way. After all the rocks are in, the cedar bag comes out, then the antlers. Then the drums come in, then the water, the dipper, then you."

He glanced at me and nodded his head and looked at the ground like he was getting it. Almost all the people were in, and I turned to go. "Wait a minute," he said, grabbing my arm. "Could you go over that for me one more time?"

"Ok." He was a soft-skinned, round-headed, intellectual type, and memorized the procedure, his eyes scanning rapidly back and forth behind his round, wire-rimmed glasses. All those kids at camp were mostly straight-A students. Bright kids. Mostly fortunate, mostly east coast kids, most of whom had never

ever swung an axe. Coming out here and sleeping in tipis was a good experience for them.

I told him if he had any problems, we'd prompt him from the lodge. "Your left brain, linear thinking shuts down around here. You probably won't be able to count to seven."

He chuckled nervously at the apparent joke, but his expression said, "I may not know anything about what we're doing here, but I sure know how to count to seven."

His intelligence had been insulted. "That's okay," I told him. "It happens to everybody."

Just as I was about to enter, he asked, "First seven, then the pipe comes out, right?"

"Right," I told him, and went in.

He picked up the cedar bag with a questioning look. I nodded and he passed it in. Then the antlers, then the pipe. Then he went back to the fire and made sounds like he was surprised the job was as hot as it was and laboriously brought the stones to the lodge. After the fifth stone, he leaned close to the door and whispered, "How many is that?"

Who's in the Circle

In that circle, inside the arbor, we've got leaders and we've got followers. There are Indians, white people, mixed-bloods, and full-bloods. There are Lakotas, Mohawks, Cree, Blackfeet, Cheyenne, Taino, Cherokee, Part-Cherokee, Some-Cherokee, and one Pawnee guy, by God.

There are Irish, Germans, Mexicans, Englishmen, and Filipinos, and a Mayan traditional Daykeeper. There are holy men and medicine men and crooks and thieves. There are big people and little people, tree huggers and lumberjacks.

There are doctors and killers, lawyers and known felons. There are could've-beens, oughta-bees, wannabees, and desperados. There are mechanics and artists, new-agers and movie stars.

There are accountants and psychologists, teachers and students. There's plumbers and businessmen, contractors and bikers. There are electricians, musicians, performing artists and scam artists. There are the loud and boastful, and the humble and quiet.

There are Vietnam vets and guys from Korea and the Gulf. There's a person who hasn't had a drink in fifteen years, and another who was drinking just the other night. There are people on meds, on caffeine, on pot, and others who smoke cigarettes throughout the Dance. There are parents, grandparents, great grandparents, and a full-blood Lakota kid who's in grade school.

There are journalists and the pitiful, academics and degenerates. There are people making six figures and others on welfare. There's a truck driver, a deer hunter, a bounty hunter, and a physical fitness nut.

There are people with big egos, and people with big hearts.

There are people who haven't sweat since last year, and those who sweat last night. There's that one who's been ready for a year, and that other one still working on his eagle-bone whistle. There are people who don't know nuthin', and that other guy over there who knows it all.

And then there are all sorts of therapists and healers.

I think it was a fellow dancer, David Frankel, to whom I said, "There sure are a lot of healers in camp this year."

David replied, "Yeah. There are about forty-five of them in the arbor."

Warrior Culture

The Lakota are a warrior culture. If you've read any of the history, you already know that. Crazy Horse was probably the most well known. Sitting Bull was a medicine man and present at the battle of the Little Big Horn (Greasy Grass), but he didn't participate in the fighting.

He was a visionary and told The People they'd win.

Acquisition of the horse helped a lot. Horses, the Sunka Wakan (sacred dog), helped the Lakota rule a territory from Canada south to the North Platte, and from the Missouri west to the Tetons. That's a pretty big stretch of turf, encompassing what is now Nebraska, Minnesota, North and South Dakota, Wyoming, and Montana. They were feared and respected by their neighbors.

So, historically, the Oglala Lakota, as the books say, "were a fierce and war-like people." Some people around here say Indians were peaceful before the arrival of the white man, but they were fighting then for the same reasons men fight today—control over a piece of real estate. Just ask the Crows, the Blackfeet, or Pawnees.

Or you could ask the Hidatsa, Mandans, Assiniboin, Cheyenne, or Arapahoe, although there was some intermarrying and alliances among some of these tribes. Point is, the Lakota were respected by their neighbors for their fierce, warlike ways, much like the U.S. is viewed today by the Canadians and Mexicans.

That's why the Lakota were so pissed about the de facto theft of the Black Hills, and still are today. The Hills were never sold or exchanged by treaty. The warriors were overwhelmed by sheer numbers. Gold seekers, bartenders, bankers, outlaws, and tramps. Like locusts, they said. The old maps say "Unceded Indian Territory."

But what the hell does that mean? If it's not ceded, then it still belongs to them, doesn't it? Stoled, not sold.

For Indians, the treaties are still an open issue. 1868 just happened yesterday.

That's what the people right up the road at Oglala will tell you. They say Oglala had more warriors per capita during Vietnam than any other place in the country. Oglala wasn't the birthplace of AIM, the American Indian Movement, but it was the birthplace of a lot of defiant AIM-sters, home of the shoot-out with the feds, and birthplace of the drive-by shooting. Oglala is thick-full of warriors, as is Pine Ridge Reservation in general. And for that matter, all of Indian Country is full of warriors.

You'd think that after the historical treatment received at the hands of the U.S. government, Indians would be the very last people to fight for this country, but contrarily, Indians are the first to enlist. There's honor in being a warrior, and at every powwow across Indian Country, the warriors are recognized before the party begins. The warriors and the flag make the circuit before the grand entry.

And if you're from a warrior culture and there's a war going on, you're going to go be in it. Whereas in the larger culture, a man might wish to hide the fact he was a Vietnam vet, here in Indian Country, the guys wear their branch of service like a billboard on the front of their caps. Korea, WWII, Vietnam, and the Gulf.

Warrior vets are everywhere.

The warriors were back in the Black Hills today. Their broken-down war ponies were sitting in the huge asphalt parking lot. If they were on foot, a shuttle would pick them up, take them in, and return them home to the reservation.

His patches on the back of his jacket were a declaration as he sat waiting for his appointment. From the back, he looked like a whole man. A long pony tail draped over a blue jean jacket with the sleeves cut off into a vest. A sewn-on patch said "Vietnam Vet," with the years he was there and his unit. You've seen his black patch for the MIAs proclaiming, "You Are Not Forgotten."

When he looked up, I flashed him a sharp salute. His tired face of pain registered momentary surprise.

"I saw your patches from the back. Welcome home, Brother."

"Thank you," he said, shaking my extended hand, then added awkwardly in a voice welling with waver, "It's appreciated."

Enough said. No need for extended conversation. The connection.

Enough said. He knows. I know.

Enough said.

In another wing of the big, sprawling, octopus-like maze of the Black Hills VA hospital at Hot Springs, there were more vets shuffling around. Not too many young ones. Mostly older guys walking with canes and in wheelchairs and pushing around little green oxygen tanks with plastic tubes running up their noses.

On the wards of the domiciliary, lost warriors lay on beds in eight-by-ten-foot cubicles, flat on their backs and staring up at the ceiling. Who knows why they were there and not with a family somewhere. All their belongings were neatly arranged within their personal space. There were rules on the wards.

Somewhere someone was shooting an angry game of pool by himself in a day room, the balls clacking loudly in echoes off the tombstone walls. Other vets meandered the halls with that crazy-ward ghost shuffle. All the staff walked. All the vets were limping or shuffling or wheeling their way through the spic-and-span catacomb corridors. Some shuffled along with a glazed look in their eyes, like they never really came home at all.

Some made momentary eye contact with a nod of their heads.

Down in the ground-level canteen, outpatient warriors shuffled along the lunch line, pushing their trays down the stainless steel tubular counter in front of the Wednesday special, chicken and rice soup. The staff were seated three and four to a table, bantering excitedly among themselves, while eyeing the vets with looks of apprehension.

The warriors were quiet and eating one-to-a-booth, their unmistakable look of lonely, tired despair reflecting their prolonged experience in obtaining post-war medical treatment from the government. Some still had that vacant, "one-thousand-yard stare" that they brought home with them. Some had colostomy bags.

Some had hooks for hands. Some had their refilled medications partially protruding from their pockets in clear plastic bags. "If you live long enough, you'll eventually end up on meds," Dr. Dave once said.

I was safe behind sunglasses while awaiting a travel voucher to be printed out by a nice lady at a computer who asked a series of rigorous, but polite questions. "You came over from . . . ?"

"Pine Ridge."

"You're still in Oglala?" she asked.

"Yes."

"It says here, 'Purple Heart' . . . are you here for your . . . ?"

"No," I told her, resisting the urge to holler out loud, "My mind!" just to get everyone in the place to look up.

"You, uh . . . saw . . . Dr. K. today?" she asked quietly, looking up, her words trailing off to a bare, sensitive whisper as she glanced over my shoulder at a Korean War vet in a blue windbreaker with an aluminum cane and one good foot.

"Yes."

Plastered on the walls were posters proclaiming "Every Day is Veteran's Day," and "Proud to Serve," and signs with arrows indicating where the "Pink Team" had been moved. A thin man with a thin moustache across a sarcophagus face, Copenhagen teeth, and black cowboy boots three sizes too large walked loudly on his heels on the polished floor, pushing a large janitorial dust mop. The Korean vet with one good foot stepped back against the wall to let him pass.

Over at the cashier's window, a genuinely pleasant woman counted out my travel reimbursement through a four-inch hole in her Plexiglass window. "There's one . . . two . . . three . . . and four. Twenty-five . . . fifty . . . seventy-five . . . six . . . seven . . . and eight. That's not much," she said, pushing four bucks and twenty-eight cents into a stainless steel tray under the Plexiglass.

"Couple gallons of gas," I told her. She said, "Have a nice day," as I shuffled away.

— — — — —

To mark the official start of the powwow, they called all the vets into the circle. "WWII, Korea, Vietnam, or the Gulf," cried the announcer. "Man or woman . . . in uniform or out . . . c'mon out here."

We lined up behind the flag, shook hands with each other, then circled the arena doing a two-step to the drum.

Old men, young boys, women, young girls, some in uniform, home on leave.

We marched. The drum resounded in my chest, my heart in my throat as we passed the crowd in step to the drum. In slow motion we passed. Old ladies bringing their hands together in slow motion, mouthing a silent, unheard "Thank you." Passing smiling, loving faces in slow motion, kids on dads' shoulders, hands clapping in slow motion, more horrendous than a dream. My heart was throbbing in my ears, the drum muffled. Blood rushed to my head. I was drenched in sweat, eyes locked ahead, trying to keep from crying.

As we marched around the circle, about halfway around, right past those old ladies, the guy in front of me, a white guy who looked like he served in the 'Nam, broke ranks and ran, rushing through the crowd toward the exit doors, never looking back.

Feeling About Writing

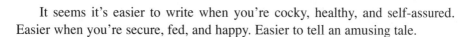

It seems it's easier to write when you're cocky, healthy, and self-assured. Easier when you're secure, fed, and happy. Easier to tell an amusing tale.

The flipside is insecurity, homelessness, and hunger. You still get to live, but not with quite the same quality of life. And it's hard to hammer out a story under a bridge. The story is there, but you've got to carry it around in your head until the opportunity affords itself to put it down onto paper or into a machine.

Like a commentary on civilization, it's hard to teach philosophy to a hungry man. For art to flourish, certain basic preconditions of life must first be met. Hard to produce an oboe concerto on an empty stomach.

Like my Sun Dance brother Mike Afraid of Bear used to shout with joy after finishing a meal, "I'M GONNA LIVE!"

And like these half-breed mutts that hang around here, and the rez dog in general, life on many Indian reservations will teach something about the life of a desperado. Desperado mutts. Feast or famine. Not just the dogs, but many of the people who live here. Loretta once said, "If all these people who want to be Indians knew how hard it was, they wouldn't want any part of it."

I've heard more than once, "It's hard to be an Indian."

That's the price of staying here. You've got to take everything that comes with it, and to understand it, you've got to live it. Sometimes, you have to leave to live. You might wonder, then why would anyone possibly want to live here?

That's what poverty does to people. Like a prison stretch or debilitating injury, it changes your view of who you are, where you're going, and even who you used to be. You live the helplessness, dependency, depression, and hopelessness. One day bleeds into the next. You stop looking in mirrors and attending to anything beyond routine personal hygiene.

"You could use a haircut, Dad," my son Digger told me during a visit, reaching up and playfully flicking the hair growing low, down on the back of my neck. "You're startin' to look like the freaking Yeti."

A look in the mirror for the first time in weeks confirmed his observation. "AIIIIIEEEEEEEE."

"Yeah," he laughed, teasing. "You're startin' to look like the freakin' Sasquatch."

So later, after a shave and a haircut with a set of clippers, my daughter Mia cleaned up the back of my neck.

Then here, last week, specifically for cosmetic purposes and concern about a mole under my left eye that appeared to have grown since the last two Sun Dances and prolonged exposure this summer to the sun, I got a surgical scalpel and . . . some box cutters, by God . . . and set about removing this dark spot from my face.

Quit twice, thinking that maybe a real doctor should check it out. But no, proceeded straight ahead with what you could call "out patient treatment." Froze it first. No. Washed my hands first. Then, remembering that Keith said he had his frozen off by a dermatologist, I went outside and got some ice, then came in and froze it.

So, if you've got any spots like this that you'd like to remove, that would be my suggestion. Freeze it first.

Next part was a little more complicated, but essentially, all that's involved is the removal of tissue.

At one point, it was sort of painful, and like I said, I quit. More than sort of. It was downright acute. Then I tried again, and quit again, reeling away gasping, "MY GOD," when feeling what I was pulling at was attached to nerves running under my eye, across my cheek under the cheekbone, and down toward the corner of my mouth. It was giving me the yim yams.

The third time . . . with the scalpel, since the box cutter was too big and awkward for the job, I finally finished the exploratory and excavation part, taking extreme care not to poke myself in the eye, since everything in the mirror was bass ackwards. Trimmed up the remaining skin fragments with toenail clippers.

A down-home, reservation-style, outpatient surgical procedure, not unlike my screaming circumcision, delicately performed at home by my dad when I was about three or four—a memory successfully repressed for about forty years until one day when I was in a pharmacy and got a whiff of camphor.

A medicine man once said the pool of saliva under our tongue is a natural antibiotic. That's why when we cut our finger, the first thing we do is put it in our mouth. Dogs got it too, he said. A natural medicine. At the time, there weren't any dogs around to lick it, and I had no camphor, so I used my own spit. It stung, but it felt right.

After a few days the bruise from the traumatized area around the . . . injury . . . it wasn't just a mole anymore . . . began to heal. I checked it out, and, by God, it looked okay. In fact, it turned out so successful that I'm thinking about removing another one, in a more difficult and less public area.

"Yes, Doctor. It could be a difficult procedure," as they say.

Just right now, on the Sunday afternoon show on KILI Radio, "The Voice of The Lakota Nation" (recognized as the best Indian-owned radio station in the country), they're playing some really fine powwow music by Blacklodge, Stoney Park, Northern Cree Singers, and others. Somebody called in complaining, asking about "playing something else," like rap, I suppose.

Anyway, the DJ told them over the air that they could turn the channel if they didn't like it. After the next song, he thanked all the people who called the station in appreciation of the music, and told the audience his show was preserving Lakota culture. And for all those people who love good powwow music, "WE'RE GONNA BE PLAYING IT STRAIGHT THROUGH TILL SIX O'CLOCK," he said with determination and pride.

People called throughout the following song, thanking him. Mostly elders. The DJ later played some honoring songs and expressed condolences to the families of the four rez fatalities that occurred over the weekend.

And since there's sweat lodge tonight, I got up at dawn, thinking about feeding "the boys" tonight and greeting the sun before it disappeared through a crack in a sky covered with thick, gray, ominous clouds.

Thawed some commodity burger, busted open commod tomatoes, tomato sauce, and red kidney beans, and tossed them in a pot with onions, garlic, and chili pepper, along with a green bell pepper I got from Sandy, and mixed up a big pot of commodity chili.

Made some commodity cornbread from scratch . . . not that that's anything complicated . . . and a batch of commodity oatmeal and raisin cookies. Got cinnamon and brown sugar from Sandy, too, but the rest was all commods.

I'm happy to have the commodities . . . they'll get you by, though it's far from "fine dining." Outside, a biting wind is howling, like it has been all day, blowing the fur flat against the ribs of the rez dogs, walking sideways and leaning into the wind that back-drafted intolerable smoke into my tiny cabin, which Poncho says he'll probably need back in a couple of weeks, since he's expecting to be leaving his current residence.

That's what prompted me to use the oven. Not Poncho . . . the intolerable smoke. Had to empty live coals into a galvanized tub outside and air out the cabin. Needed the oven for heat. Then, while I was over at Sandy's getting the cinnamon and brown sugar and bell pepper, the wind pulled some of those ashes out of the tub and set to smolder some straw and wood chips right there under the porch. My pile of wood ten rows deep, twenty-five feet long, and six feet high was a mere fifteen feet away.

It's a good thing I came home when I did. Otherwise Poncho might have questioned why I burned down his cabin. It would be highly suspect, since he was just here yesterday. If it was me, I'd wonder if I did it just in spite. Such things have been known to occur around here.

Nah. That's not my style. I'm more inclined to take off to somewhere remote and act like I'm never coming back. Sell everything off for the tickets. I've got a thousand-dollar woodpile and a buffalo robe that should easily fetch a round-trip ticket to Hong Kong, which, incidentally, these days you can go British Airways for $265 out of New York. Since that box cutter incident, they're begging people to fly.

Anyway, it's easier to tell an amusing tale when you're fed, secure, and self-assured. I'm fed, because I've been dipping into that chili; but because of the aforementioned anticipated eviction, I'm not too secure right now. It's January, for Christ's sake.

I've tasted homelessness in February before. It's unsettling, like two years up here in a tipi.

None of that is secure. It gets a person thinking about drifting down toward Mexico or the Caribbean. Someplace warm. Then why, you might ask, would anybody want to live here?

Larue once told us, "When you make that prayer, move forward knowing it's already being answered. Don't let doubt enter into your mind." In the dynamics of psychology, it's defined as what they refer to as the power of self-fulfilling prophecy. In religion, it's faith.

And so, last night, I went out and sparked up the lodge, sitting out a hundred yards east of the cabin, lined up with the ancient volcano, Maki Zita. I waited around awhile for someone else to show up, like the Cherokee princess, but she didn't, so I went in by myself.

Just now, it's late afternoon. The wind let up, and the sun, plunging toward the horizon, temporarily broke through the bank of heavy snow clouds on the western horizon, filled the cabin with light, and drenched Maki Zita and the buttes off to the east with a golden glow.

The four rez dogs, lounging around on the deck out of the wind and full on chili, cornbread, commodity cheese, and oatmeal cookies, looked over their shoulders and smiled a tongue-lolling thank you, their eyes filled with gratitude.

Dancer's Lodge

Needed to be in three places at the same time yesterday. Oglala post office a half hour north, Chadron State College Chess Tournament representing Slim Buttes, and back here at 3:00 p.m. to light the fire for the dancer's lodge.

Sent my clone to Oglala and went in person to the chess tournament, since the organizer invited me and paid my entry fee. Breezed through the first three rounds in ten minutes of the ninety allotted per game. Ran up against the number one seed and last year's reigning champ in the semifinals and conceded after blundering late in the middle game.

I did, however, beat him on the clock. I used only ten minutes, and he took twenty-seven. He brought his clock, notepad, and computer, and recorded and studied each move. I played quick and reckless and used only a ballpoint pen, which I brought along as a psychological device and kept clicking while he pondered his moves, a strategy I learned from the Russians.

If I'd stretched the game out for thirteen more minutes, I could have won under the agreed forty minutes we set for the game, but I needed to get back out here on the treacherous, drift-filled Slim Buttes Road.

Big Mikey had already shoveled the lodge grounds clear of a foot of snow by the time I got home, with Tom Cook and Ron Bates right on my tail, or trail. Ron came up from Colorado in a station wagon, which he gave to Ernest, laughing in delight at the giveaway.

Tom, driving the green, battered, four-wheel-drive pickup "Thunder," went over the hill to check on Loretta and Beatrice, while Ron, Big Mikey, and I pulled dry wood from my pile, stacked the rocks, and lit the fire. Lost count of the rocks, somewhere around fifteen, so we used all twenty-eight from the last lodge, and since some of them were little, we added about ten or twelve big, fresh ones. It was gonna be a hot one.

We have a joke about how many rocks we use (normally, twenty-seven), and when anyone asks, "How many rocks?" we say, "All of 'em . . . plus two."

Everything out at the lodge was wet, muddy, and sloppy, so Ron and I brought the dump truck La Roja back to the house for another hour's worth of dry wood. Right then came Perry Stamp from Kansas and Roy Reddeman from up north of Milwaukee, riding with Lou Redman from down in Torrington, Wyoming.

Right behind them, in Sandy's car, came the guys from Colorado . . . Sandy and Rob Stuart, both of whom worked as firemen at last year's Dance. I remember Rob saying at the fire last year, "I'm new. I don't know anything. I'm here to help. Don't worry about offending me."

For newcomers, that sort of humble approach is good and sits well with everyone.

All those guys brought three or four gallons of juice, two kinds of chicken, salmon, buffalo stew, chicken and rice soup, Pepsi, oranges, potato salad, cheese, and a double-chocolate flat cake with blue icing, balloons, and a rez dog on it.

They also brought really good, clean energy with them, along with generally good cheer. We hadn't seen each other since the Dance.

Ernest showed up and greeted everyone individually with a hearty, "HEYYYYYYY." He stayed up here at the house drinking coffee and visiting with Ron, while the rest of us joined Big Mikey, who was staying with the fire.

We all went out to the lodge and joked, smoked, and threw snowballs, trying to see who could hit La Roja, sitting about ten feet away. Lou brought a bag of cedar, little cigars, and and a sack full of amusing tales—dancers standing around smoking cigars and laughing—man, we were in hog heaven.

We saw Joe American Horse from a distance, walking down the drive. "Is that Tom?" someone asked.

"No. He's walking too fast," said Lou. "Looks like Uncle Joe."

It was. He'd gotten stuck, left Timmy in the car, and walked the half mile back here to the house. Big Mikey left immediately to go pull him out. "I got stuck in front of Blind Man's, but I didn't want to go over there, so I walked back," he explained later.

Ron and the Old Man came back to the fire, and we were all there, waiting for Tom, and maybe Henry Red Cloud, and maybe Owen Warrior, who said he was coming.

Out of the blue the Old Man said, "When we came home from New York, I went up to the door and knocked." He made a knocking motion with his hand. "It's me," he said. "I'm home."

Speaking for his imaginary girlfriend, he says, "Yer clothes are out on the deck."

"Eeeeeeeee," he said. "'Yer clothes are out there'" . . . "I heard you the first time."

Everybody just laughed along with him as he made fun of himself and his moody, contentious girlfriend.

"I heard you the first time," Lou repeated, laughing, and said, "Man, you'll never run out of material with this guy around," nodding toward the Old Man.

Tom arrived and greeted all the out-of-town dancers with a warm "Welcome home," and we loaded the Sun Dance pipe.

About dark, we went in. Eleven of us. I brought the stones and Sandy caught them.

We sang seven songs the first round, then four through each of the remaining three rounds. It's hard to believe that a seventy-seven year-old man can knock down us younger men. Several of the guys . . . won't say who . . . were begging for mercy, crying for the door to be opened, some squeaking out a faint, "Mitakuye Oyasin," while others shouted it out, "MITAKUYE OYASIN!" Even heard Uncle Joe let out a rare "heyyYYYHHH."

Didn't open it up until the Old Man finished praying and called for it hisself.

Smoked the Sun Dance pipe after the third door, and it stayed lit all the way around . . . a good sign. Between doors, a few of the guys mentioned special prayers and talked good to Tom and the old men about their guidance and leader-ship. Generally speaking, everyone expressed gratitude.

Finished up, came out, and everybody was red-faced, refreshed, and joyous. A really good one.

We all reconvened here at the house, joked around, ate really good, and recovered. The Old Man said he needed to get home to stay out of the doghouse, and drove off in his new car after saying he wanted to go ahead with today's lodge. Then Joe and Timmy left.

"You staying around for a few more days?" we asked Roy.

He shook his head. "No. I'm headed back tomorrow."

Eleven hundred plus miles. Drove out from Milwaukee, took in a sweat lodge, then headed back. Perry headed back to Kansas. The guys from Colorado took off for their five-hour drive.

Big Mikey said he'd be up in the morning for a buffalo stew breakfast and left. Tom and I sat here in the quiet for awhile. The rez dogs snacked on chicken bones and buffalo stew left in Styrofoam bowls.

"The Old Man wants to sweat again TOMORROW?" Tom asked.

"Yeah."

"Aiehh," we both expressed in an exhausted expulsion of breath.

Another good sign—when the cedar smudge can was going around before we went in, Joe smudged Timmy, who is customarily unresponsive to most everything. This time, Timmy pulled off his hooded sweatshirt so his head could be smudged, and Lou said he heard him say something.

Gumbo Country

It's a good thing us folks out here in the country really didn't need to go anywhere yesterday, today, or tomorrow. After that foot of snow last week that shut everything down, our above-freezing temperatures of the past three days have melted nearly all the snow, except for patches here and there and the shrinking mounds left-over from people digging out. There were just a couple of days there, between the storm and the melt-off, that we could get out.

"City folks don't ever have to do this," said a friend as we laid down several long wooden plank walkways and flat sheets of plywood across the morass of mud around the deck. Most Americans get to live on concrete. Homes on concrete slabs attached to a garage on a concrete slab where their car sits.

The garage lets out onto a concrete driveway leading to a concrete street, and like most Americans, people drive to three places: work, the gas station, and the grocery store. At the grocery store, there's a concrete parking lot. At the gas station, they pull onto another slab of concrete. At work, there's another concrete parking lot and a building atop more concrete. Maybe just outside there'll be some manicured grass. Maybe not.

Point is, most people in America never get mud on their shoes. When's the last time? Farmers and country folk know what I'm talking about. Most people, when you say "Gumbo," are thinking shrimp Creole or Cajun catfish, but up here on Pine Ridge, when you say "gumbo," we're talking MUD with a bold-faced, capital "**M**."

Out here in "the sticks," the closest concrete would be . . . geeeee . . . Pine Ridge Village, I guess.

The seat of civilization. There's no sidewalks anywhere in Pine Ridge, but there's concrete streets.

There's pavement about a mile from here, which most people hope to "make it" to when they leave here, after slithering and sliding and flinging mud out of two inescapable tire ruts, creeping along on a white-knuckle prayer at seven miles per hour while the speedometer says you're going sixty.

"I sure hope I can make it to the pavement," people will say.

People will call ahead before coming out and ask about the road conditions. "Can I make it back there?" they'll ask. "What's the road like?"

Road? Road? Is that what you call it?

"Stay off the road. Take the alternate. If it's impassable, take the sub-alternate. If the sub-alternate is closed, stay on the grass. After that, you're on your own."

What we end up with each spring is a Ho Chi Minh Trail series of rutted spider routes fanning out from the pavement and converging on our homes. By the time you get here, your vehicle will be covered in mud, with Slim Buttes gumbo packed up under the wheel wells and entire undercarriage, especially if you've got front wheel drive.

When you go into Chadron, Nebraska, you can easily tell the Indian cars from the reservation. "There's a rez ride," people will note of a mud-caked car with South Dakota plates.

Despite the prevailing conditions that are keeping me in, there have been a houseful of visitors, all at the same time, all of whom arrived in four-wheel drive vehicles—Aloysius, Bryan and his attorney from Boston, Steve, who remarked, "Gee, you can see for miles out here." He also commented on his arrival, "Why is that dog on your porch?"

"Keeping watch. He's a watchdog."

Then Tom Cook, Manuel Martin, Bo and Misty Sioux Davis, Sal Lame, and another guy arrived from down over the hill where they were working on a greenhouse, all of 'em spinning and slurping around in the fresh mud, rerouting the four man-hour ditch constructed to divert the runoff to the garden, instead of the driveway. Everyone tromped in, looking for a cup of coffee.

"Can I borrow your rifle?" Misty asked. "There's a whole pack of dogs every morning chasing my dog around. She's in heat."

"You gonna shoot 'em?"

"No. Just scare 'em off."

"I don't know about sending a gun over to your trailer."

"It's okay," she said. "My kids know about guns."

"I'm not worried about the kids," I replied. "It's the adults I'm concerned about."

They all sat around for awhile, visiting and reading last week's news and drinking coffee—fixed seven or eight pots—and talked about a little bit of everything before all heading out at the same time, leaving mud all over the floor. Wet mud, dry mud, thick mud, watery mud, and caked mud. Misty was the only one who removed her boots.

Here, and it seems throughout Indian Country, the mop bucket is a semipermanent fixture and another aspect of gumbo life that most Americans don't have to think about or deal with. We keep an active mop bucket just inside the door for days like this, and mop the floor five, six, seven, eight times a day, since few people remove their boots when entering your home.

"OH! Sorry," they'll sometimes say when they see all the mud they've tracked into the house, leaving a trail from the door to the woodstove to the coffee pot to the kitchen table.

"That's okay. No problem. I've got a mop."

It's okay, but after two seasons of constant mopping during weather like this, the floor tiles have begun to lift from the subflooring on the high-traffic areas just inside the door, over by the stove, over by the coffeepot, and over by the kitchen table.

So, you can actually get in and out of here once the ground freezes. That's an hour or so after sunset, and again in the morning before sunrise, and about an hour after it comes up. Once it begins to thaw, we're back to the soupy, sloppy conditions of the day before.

So, once the ground thaws out, I can bury Fuzz, who's lost a lot of weight but still looks intimidating standing stiff-legged up on the deck, facing south, the direction people come from to approach the door. Despite the weight loss, he can still stand up, since he's pretty rigid now, it's been almost a week since he was "put down," or executed, by my neighbor, Marvin Goings.

Nevertheless, he still sort of serves his purpose as a guard dog, keeping the other dogs off the deck and forcing visitors to walk around him, although he can't give me notice or warning of approaching company anymore. His voice is out.

So, two things start to occur when the sun comes out. First, the ground starts to thaw, making the drive back here a real challenge; and second, depending on the direction of the breeze, that dog starts to stink. Gotta keep an eye on the thermometer, and a nose out for the direction of the wind.

Hospitals, Ceremonies, and Cemeteries

When we entered Tom and Loretta's house in Chadron, Lupe, in the commanding and authoritative manner of a bailiff, said to the nine men gathered there, "All rise."

Everybody laughed. We needed a laugh. It had been two weeks since Ernest's stroke, and he still remained at the VA hospital in Hot Springs, slowly recovering his speech and movement on the right side of his body. Can't swallow. They took him to Fort Mead and had a tube installed to his stomach for direct feeding. Nothing around the kitchen was the same, and the air hung with a palpable sadness.

The daughter of another relative was brain-dead after a car wreck, they said, so they pulled the plug. Another cousin was diagnosed with cancer, and somebody else associated with the family up and died of a heart attack at thirty-some years old. And then the daughter of "Grandma Celeste" also died of a heart attack.

Our only teenage Sun Dancer, Jack Red Cloud, pulled out onto the highway coming out of Cheyenne Creek and got hit head-on by some high-schoolers, and he ended up in the hospital in Rapid City all smashed up.

Then just before all this, Loretta's back went out, leaving her in excruciating enough pain for an emergency run to Rapid City, and Beatrice was in and out of the hospital just days before for some kind of a thing. And Poncho just now called and said another granny had died.

"Something is hitting this family hard," Aloysius said here the other night.

Accordingly, in Indian Country, there's all sorts of unsolicited speculation from most everyone about the cause-effect relationship attributed to the occurence of anything negative. This spirit did this, and that spirit did that, and this happened because that person didn't do something just right, or somebody's grandmother seven generations ago forgot to put something out, or that person from the grave is putting some kind of mojo on us.

It's bewildering at times, and one wonders how all these various opinions can be right. "Well, if it's that spirit of that guy who died along the creek ten or fifteen years ago, then what about ignoring a doctor's advice to stop smoking cigarettes and drinking coffee?" And what about a lifetime of commodities, fry bread, and tanega?

The car wrecks? That's a whole nuther thing. I don't know.

So now, people are praying for the old man. "The doctors are doing what they can do, but we've got to try our Indian medicine, too," Aloysius said. So Al has been over to doctor Ernest three times now, using a spirit medicine and "Indian doctoring." Tonight, he used it with Beatrice and Loretta and I there in the room. The old man responded to it. We were encouraged.

"The white man has his ways of healing that he believes in, and we have ours," Al said.

So it seems everybody is running back and forth between hospitals, ceremonies, and cemeteries.

So there in the kitchen at Tom's house, we all needed something to laugh about.

Coming in from the districts, all the tractor drivers were gathered around the table, strewn with time sheets, looking to get paid since Tom just got back from Hawaii, where he and Loretta went for a week to see their kids.

Uncle Joe was also there, along with Johnson Bear Robe, his son, Johnson, and Gooksie Red Bear, and Mike Red Bear, and Whatshisname from Oglala. Duane Locke and Clayton Dempsey were there from Porcupine. About eight or nine guys in the house, chatting, drinking coffee, messing with the cat. Loretta was with her mom over in Hot Springs, seeing Ernest. The phone kept ringing. Incoming. Felt almost like a siege. More people arriving at the door. Fix another pot of coffee.

All the heavy stuff came down just when Tom and Loretta left, diving under the radar for a week before returning to deal with the intensity of where they left off, and the upcoming Sun Dance, now a month away. "It was good to take a break," Loretta said at the hospital. "We needed to get away."

In Ernest's absence, Uncle Joe ran sweat, a little bit awkwardly and cool enough for the boys to ask him to turn it up on high next time. Aloysius put up peyote meeting for Mother's Day and Beatrice's seventy-fifth birthday, calling on Darrell and Rusty Red Cloud to prep the ceremony and trying to pull everything together right up to the last minute.

He pulled it off, and ran the ceremony himself after his "roadman" got bogged down, broke down over in Rosebud, and his back-up, Alfred Red Cloud, was sick. Uncle Emerson Spider showed up, along with Kurt Fool Bull, some Navajos, and enough local relatives for a full tipi, and a big crowd turned out the next day for the feed, including me and Grant, a dancer from Colorado who was up for the weekend, but declined on taking in the meeting.

"I not sure I can handle that peyote right now," he said. "And if I'm not sure, then I probably shouldn't go in."

High Times editor Malcolm MacKinnon, who was here from New York to shoot the annual horse races up at Alex White Plume's, said pretty much the same thing when Aloysius invited him to "take in" and shoot the meeting for the record. He was all excited about shooting the meeting, but changed his mind at the last minute and headed back to the east coast.

And the "Kentucky Boys," Craig Lee and "Red," were here, hanging around with Henry and going up to Manderson to see Alex about hemp-related business, I think, but they too headed out suddenly, declining on Aloysius' invite to take in the meeting. Well, like they say, it isn't for everybody.

Grant and I walked over the hill, where the meeting was being held on the grounds outside of Beatrice's "Old Place." It was 10:30 p.m., the sun long down. No drum. No fire. Where was everybody? We came back over the hill.

Around midnight Saturday, everybody showed up, and they sang throughout the night and well into the next morning. After preparing the sweat fire and putting on two hours' worth of ash wood, Grant and I went over for the first breakfast of water, corn, meat, and chokecherry wasna. Everyone was all "peyotied up" and glowing goodness, including Bryan Lockwood, a high school friend from Massachusetts, taking in his first peyote meeting.

"I got sick and finally threw up," he said. "After that, I was okay."

Yeah. That's what they say.

Raymondo Eagle Bear, our young Sun Dancer who danced the full four years over in the canyon, also attended the meeting with his Fool Bull relatives from Rosebud Reservation and came with us back over the hill, riding in the back of "La Roja," La Roja Grande, our big red five-ton dump truck. Raymondo brought good cheer to the gathering here as he shot baskets in the kitchen with a nerf ball and laughed with the carefree glee of a kid at ease around grownups.

He said he got good grades this year and passed on to the seventh grade. He said he'd be dancing with us again next month.

About a dozen men came over the hill to a good hot sweat that Aloysius ran, then we all went back over for the main meal of chicken, turkey, hamburgers, hot dogs, potato salad, macaroni salad, fry bread, candy salad, coffee, Kool Aid, lemonade, beef soup, dried meat soup, and a couple other serious-looking vats of tanega, or tripe, or tub-of-stroke that the people all love, and that they know is killing them, but they can't get enough of.

"You relatives take this food home," Aloysius announced. "Don't leave anything. Take it with you. Share it around. We don't want to take anything back inside."

Out came the watecha (take home) buckets. Tupperware, coffee cans, all sorts of containers.

There was ice cream and cake, too. About five or six different cakes, and the old lady had a really nice birthday. Five or six people shot photos. Jack Red Cloud showed up, too, out of the hospital and moving reeeeeally slow.

It's amazing how fast a crowd breaks up after they've been fed.

Tipi came down, the women cleaned up, and people headed for their cars.

"I'm thinking about a hot shower and a bed," said Bryan, clearly dragging ass, just like everybody else who took in meeting. He didn't feel like taking in another sweat with the regular Sunday night crowd. Calling an east phone friend, he said, "Life is good here, but it's really HARD."

"None of the peyote people are going to make it," I said to Uncle Joe as we watched the sun set, sort of waiting for Ernest to come driving up. "We might as well go ahead on in."

Ernest has been difficult to understand, and isn't talking much, but last week he said in English, "Continue . . . the . . . prayer."

There were another dozen people here for the Sunday evening sweat lodge, including three youngsters. Uncle Joe brought his invalid son Timmy to sweat for one last time before turning him over to a state boarding school. He'd been talking about it for some time, and the time had finally arrived. Timmy is seventeen now, and Joe has raised him since he was about two.

"I hate to do it," Joe said. "But he's getting too much for me to handle. I'm getting too old."

Joe must have been thinking about Ernest, and his own mortality. "If something happens to me, then who's going to take care of him?" he asked. "It's probably better this way," he said.

The next day, Joe called the house. "It sure is quiet over here," he said with a laugh that betrayed his sudden loneliness. "I went into the next room, but he's not there."

La Roja Goes To Heaven

It was good to get back on "The Grounds"—the Sun Dance grounds over in the canyon on the Wild Horse Sanctuary owned by Dayton Hyde, south of Hot Springs at the southern end of the Black Hills, "He Sapa" in "Indian," as they say, or Lakota.

The land, which we call "The Holy Land," is surely sacred. It sits adjacent to Hell's Canyon, one of South Dakota's tourist attractions. Being the contrarians that we are, we began calling it "Heaven's Canyon," either out of reverence or spite. So, we know the place by a lot of different names.

"Devil's Tower . . . Hell's Canyon," Uncle Joe once told a group of young volunteers. "If the Indians thought it was sacred, the white man thought it was satanic."

Sure is peaceful up there. Sure is quiet. Two white-faced black mares approached us at the gate, wondering. Month-old paint and sorrel colts on spindly legs shied away behind their mothers, while another dozen mares raced across a pasture, running parallel to La Roja, which was loaded down with five tons of ash and cottonwood for the Dance.

Visibility was reduced to about three miles from two days of steady blow that created a dirt-filled haze that made it look like it was raining all around, except it wasn't. One of those days that leaves tiny particles of earth in your mouth and eyes. Irritating.

The Dance arbor was in a state of disrepair, as it is each year following a year's back-scratching by the horses, who don't seem to possess a sense for the sacred. Well, they were there first. Wait. No. The People were there first, weren't they?

The People brought the horses, at least in this age. The land was always holy. So were the horses. "Shunka Wakan," or "Holy Dog," they called them. Us and our pitiful little transient structures . . . "We're just scratching the surface," José Barreiro, one of our dancers said three years ago as we sat in the rocks on the canyon rim 300 feet above the Cheyenne River, snaking its way through the Black Hills. José would say the spirits of the land were there first.

First the land, then the people, then the horses, then the five-ton dump trucks. Then the developers.

Thanks to Dayton Hyde and his sense for the sacred, the developers have been kept out of the Holy Land, which is filled with petroglyphs and ancient ceremonial fire pits. We're just scratching the surface of that prehistoric land, building our pitiful arbor and doing our pitiful Dance for four days for pitiful people in a pitiful world, dancing around a magnificent tree of life.

It bent under the press of the wind, the upper branches waving and holding last year's faded prayer flags.

A set of dog tags tinkled halfway up a trunk wound with thousands of prayer ties. Dancers' ropes hung from the branches and were still gathered in a bundle on the trunk. At the base were more ties, flags, pieces of rope, cloth, and piercing pins.

There at the tree for a flash of a moment, as Lupe and his son Chachee began to unload the wood from the back of La Roja, the arbor was full of dancers. Singers around a drum, a crowd of people gathered around the arbor, tipis, and cars all around.

— — — — —

The Old Man lay sleeping when we entered his room at the VA Hospital in Hot Springs. The TV was on. Chuck Norris. Chachee paced in the hallway. When Ernest felt our presence, he woke up and pulled his left hand from under the sheets to shake our hands. He looked better.

He looked better and was talking, but he still was hard to understand. He showed us he could move both of his legs, but not his right hand yet. Getting better. He kept saying something about tomorrow, like he was coming home tomorrow, but his speech was thick and unclear.

We told him everyone wants him to come home, and everyone is praying for him, and everything was ready and waiting for him, and reminded him that we've got the Dance coming up and he's only got about three weeks now to get back on his feet and come over there and be around and run things for us.

We told him we needed him.

He nodded his head.

It looked like all those prayers and ceremonies were coming through.

He's slowly coming around. While the doctors and staff at the hospital in Hot Springs are working their magic in the physical realm, the family has been trying everything they can think of to bring about his return to good health.

Three days earlier the family had made a special request to a local medicine man and relative who conducted a healing ceremony, a puppy ceremony. The spirit helpers came, and went up there to the hospital to doctor the Old Man. A yuwipi ceremony, they said.

The medicine man said a spirit had "bumped him" (Ernest). Later we asked the professional view of what had happened from a medical doctor friend who was visiting here from California.

"He's (the medicine man) using a rattle and an eagle feather, so he's probably not going to be talking about a blocked coronary artery," he said. More than a supernatural occurrence, Dr. Tom said the stroke was likely caused by "a diet spanning a lifetime."

To complete the healing ceremony and Wopila, or Thanksgiving to the Creator for hearing our prayers, Loretta and her sister Nita fixed fry bread and a big pot of soup to feed The People.

"It's best to take care of these things right away," said Loretta as she diced up beef on her kitchen table.

"That way, our prayers will be answered right away. You don't want to put it off."

Outside, behind the house, Tom filled his pipe at his sweat lodge altar. Then we all headed west of Chadron to the medicine man's residence where they already had the fire going, the wind blowing the flame sideways. People were there from Pine Ridge, Wounded Knee, Porcupine, Slim Buttes, and Chadron. There at the fire, Leo Little Moon, a singer from Wounded Knee, talked about a rash of auto deaths that had occurred lately up that way.

Late into the evening there were about two dozen people who entered the sweat lodge, half of them women led by Beatrice and Loretta. The ceremony began and the spirits once again visited, coming in a flash of sparks and loud yakkety-yakking a thousand miles an hour in a scrambled dialogue, sounding something like a tape on fast forward, except faster. You could make out a few occasional words as they spoke in Lakota, English, and Spanish. Before they opened the door, an eagle visited the lodge and flew around in there over our heads.

"Just keep praying. That's all we can do," said Loretta. So that's what we've all been doing.

— — — — —

Just like the late day weather closing in, the ride home from Hot Springs was somber and gray following the hospital visit. The five-hour, lumbar-crunching round-trip to The Grounds and back to Pine Ridge in La Roja hammered on our spirits further.

"This was all Indian country," I said as we rolled over one hill, then another, heading east out of Buffalo Gap. Lupe just nodded sleepily, not having fully recovered from the previous night's ceremony that ended after midnight and got us home at 2:00 a.m.

The pastures and grasslands east of the Black Hills eventually yielded to the white, chalky, alkaline earth of the western end of the reservation. It was lonely and desolate out that way. No cows, no grass. Just a few pools of stagnant green water. We passed Number 6 housing district, hit the pavement finally at Loneman, and came up west of Oglala, turning south to Slim Buttes.

A front was closing in at dusk, with the advancing winds clearing the air and pushing the dust and dirt cloud off to the east. The Thunderbeings were rumbling, and light rain began pecking the windowpane.

Lightning split the air directly overhead, and two of neighbor Marvin's horses, who were over here grazing all day, laid their ears back and headed home.

When a Strange Cat Comes to Your House, Spit on It Twice

We were just sitting here talking about Aloysius' extensive knowledge of The Ways, the songs, and his intertribal affiliations with Indians across the country. As the son of both a medicine woman and medicine man, it could be supposed that he should know something about the traditional ways of The People.

His ears must have been burning . . . in a good way . . . because here he came, up over the hill.

We first noticed that black cat with the white Y on its face when the group of a dozen Landmark volunteers from Massachusetts came up from the camp down over the hill for a dinner gathering up here in the cool of the evening. We all ate together on the deck under the faint glow of strands of tiny Christmas lights strung around the frame holding the camouflage netting, installed earlier to keep the one hundred plus degree daytime heat from baking us to a crisp.

After the young volunteers left, the cat ventured timidly out from beneath the deck for food scraps that we threw out to entice it. The cat cautiously grabbed the food, then quickly retreated back under the deck. It appeared to be very hungry. Then here came Al.

Three of us sat eating sliced cantaloupe and talking in the quiet evening as the moon pushed up over the eastern horizon. At one point, Aloysius rose and went over to the edge of the deck and spat twice.

Just a few days earlier, he'd said if you're out at dark and you get a strange, creepy feeling, then you're supposed to spit on the ground, because the bad spirits don't like the smell of human spit and they'll stay away. They'll leave you alone.

"Why'd you do that?" I asked.

"Do what?" Al said.

"Why'd you spit twice on the cat?"

"Huh?" he said.

"Is it something about The Ways of The People . . . if a strange cat comes to your house, then you're supposed to spit on it twice?"

Aloysius burst out with laughter. "No," he said. "I had melon seeds in my mouth."

We laughed till it hurt. "Gotta get him TWICE!" Aloysius kept saying.

"Right in the FACE! It might be hard to get him that second time, but after that, everything's gonna be good."

"Everything's gonna be good," he said, making a palm-down cutting motion with his hand, the tears rolling from his eyes.

"I've got to go, Bro," said Al, heading toward his car.

"EEEEEEEEYAAA," he said, walking away and shaking his head. "I've gotta tell Mom about this one."

Crossing the
Auto Gate

Maybe some of you have felt it. The kids say they can feel it. Others have said so, too. It might be comparable to that sudden, queasy feeling when a plane's wheels lift off the runway, maybe with the destination to a foreign country.

But that's quite different in many respects. With flying there's a sense of being free of gravity, followed by that sickening sense, the knowledge of the possibility of falling back to earth, or at least the inevitability of returning to earth. So, that's not really being free of gravity at all. It's just an illusion of flying. One is being propelled. This is different, much different, from being on vacation.

When one enters Pine Ridge Reservation from the south on Slim Buttes Road and hits the auto gate, or "cattle guard" that marks the Nebraska/South Dakota reservation line, there's a true sense of freedom that accompanies the brrrrmp brrrrmp double-rumble of one's tires crossing the iron gate.

At times the feeling can be nearly imperceptible, particularly if you're preoccupied with obstreperous thoughts about the past or future. But if you're being in the here and now or, as sometimes can be the case, being pursued, there is an exhilarating sense of freedom when crossing onto the reservation.

Bo knows. He was home free after leading a half dozen Nebraska deputies on a high-speed chase out of White Clay, across Beaver Walls and the upper panhandle, and ending up at the rez line, whereupon someone in a uniform at an allegedly spotlit roadblock discharged six rounds from a sidearm at his fleeing truck.

SAFE! Safe at home. The catcher dropped the ball.

"It's like a big weight is lifted off your shoulders," said a friend, making an expansive gesture like he was removing a backpack. "You're leaving it all behind. It's like entering a different universe."

Welcome to Indian Country. Suddenly the land opens up and yawns out, and remote, isolated trailer houses supersede the split-level homes south of the line. Dry, parched earth and open pasturelands replace the fenced, manicured, and aquifer-fed plots of Nebraska farmers. Horses replace black angus.

Welfare-state poverty replaces productivity and the American Dream. Spirituality supplants religion. The curtain is lifted. Tight schedules yield to Indian Time.

"Out There," the frantic, manic, treadmill push. Bumper-to-bumper rush-hour fear, intrusive cell phone blather, and Banana Republic dreams. Mind-numbing media clatter chatter and chest-throbbing boom box bass beat reverberate through concrete streets, iron buildings, temple walls, and rib cages. Hurry and noise. Noise and hurry. Eighty-five miles per hour, and the impatient faster people want you over in the slow lane. The American interstate autobahn.

"What is it?" I asked the Colorado kids. "Why is it so appealing to you?"

"Up here, it's kicked back," they said.

Kicked back into time, I suppose. Kicked back into a different dimension, right here in the continental Yoo-nited States.

"I miss the stars," said a friend who'd recently returned home, east of the Mississippi. "We can't see them here."

"The wind, the stars, the fire, the steam hitting the rocks . . . the natural elements of the earth . . . that's real . . . that's the kind of freedom that people find attractive," said Milo. "The American people think they're free, but they're not," he said, sitting here over a pot of coffee.

Not really free at all. Just an illusion of freedom. Everyone is being propelled.

It's not uncommon for people to visit the reservation and become addicted to the freedom. In the past year we've witnessed friends relocate closer. "Closer to something real," they said. Closer than Los Angeles. Closer than Massachusetts. Many other visitors keep coming back.

But yet, this too is a trap, a confinement that harbors isolation and resists movement. "Five thousand square miles," said Milo. "This is the largest concentration camp in America."

Containment. We're contained. Not really free at all. Just the illusion of freedom.

Reason for Being

Sometimes I wonder what the hell I'm doing in Indian Country, sitting out here in the middle of nowhere on Pine Ridge Indian Reservation, as opposed to anywhere else in America that I'd rather not be.

Florida? Too crowded. New York? Too much. Boston? Too white. Indiana? Too backward.

North Carolina? Too redneck. California? Too bumper-to-bumper.

Colorado? Too self-righteous. Podunk, Iowa? Too lame. Texas? Ha.

Good people living in all those places, mind you. Real fine folk. But, up here feels just about right for my skin, although like anywhere you find two-leggeds, you're gonna find that "People Thing." And, as you know, "Too much peoples messes up a good thing," as Harold Leroi Johnson, an accounting student mistaken for a football player, used to say.

"When I first came here twenty-five years ago, there were no homes," the widow said, standing on her deck and looking wistfully out across a Colorado valley, filled up with obscene subdevelopment. "Now look at it."

The words came tumbling out before I could stop them. "That's what the Arapaho said when you moved in."

— — — — —

And despite the poverty and inordinate human despair that exists here, "This place is one of the best-kept secrets in America," said Milo to Gudrun, a German tourist whom we called "Gertrude" during the entirety of her month-long visit to the reservation. She corrected us only the day before she left.

Milo was her personal guide, an exceptional inner-circle access gift for a foreigner, or anybody for that matter, visiting Pine Ridge for an eye-opening experience. He took her on a thorough five-star trip: Wounded Knee, Ft. Robinson, Pine Ridge, Badlands, Mt. Rushmore, inside folk's homes . . . all up and down the line, inside out, the kind of rich, in-depth cultural encounter that German tourists and the rest of us long for when seeking a vacation beyond the superficial. A primal dose.

"This is the perfect writer's retreat," I think she said. Could've been some-one else who said it.

— — — — —

A retreat. A refuge perhaps, for refugees. Refugees of the State, contained within our own little piece of heaven, our own little piece of America, our own little concentration camp.

Five refugee children came through here yesterday, on foot. Misty's boys, Kestrel and Kassel, I think, and still can't tell who's who. They were with Josh and Eric Kills Enemy, from down on "Gaza Strip," and the boys' Aunt Ashley, Misty's younger sister, fourteen maybe sixteen years old.

They had walked the five miles over here in one hundred degree heat, arriving in the late afternoon, and sat resting on the deck under the camouflage netting. It must have seemed like an oasis. "You got anything to drink?" they asked.

"Got water . . . and some cold Pepsis."

"Pepsi, Pepsi, Pepsi, Pepsi," they all chimed.

"And one Fanta orange."

"I'll take the orange," said Ashley, turning over her Pepsi to Eric.

"Why you walking? Where's your bikes?" I asked.

Their shoulders slumped. "They've all got flats," said Kestrel, going on to explain how they tried to patch the tires with "you know . . . that white stuff," but it didn't work very well.

"We've got a pump, but it doesn't work so good," said Kassel. All the bikes were "down."

They sipped their sodas and listened attentively to how you can double up an inner tube for protection against sharp rocks and flats, before Kassel said, "We don't have no tubes . . . just that little air thing on the tire."

Reason for Being   139

They had a new dog with them, a black attack dog with a black tongue, and each one of them sang out a polite "Thank yooou," as they headed out over the hill for a dip in Tom's tank, a fifteen foot diameter, six thousand gallon, above-the-ground swimming pool for local kids and people in camp.

Besides "The Culvert," the now dried-up local swimming hole where the White River used to flow under Gaza Strip, the dirt cut-across to Pine Ridge, the only other place to swim is Cascade Falls, an hour away, south of Hot Springs. Gotta have a car. Gotta have an adult take you there.

About an hour later, they all came back over the hill and sat on the deck with graham crackers they'd discovered in the camp kitchen. Cooled off, bellies full, they were happy. There was slick, green scum on the bottom of the tank, Ashley said.

The reason they don't have no decent place to swim on a hot summer day is the same reason they don't have no decent bikes. The same reason they waited all summer for a skateboard park or ramp that didn't happen. "Why doesn't some church group . . . "

"We give out $50 billion a year in foreign aid," Milo said, "and half of that goes to the Israelis. That shows you where America's priorities lie."

— — — — —

The heat had suddenly broken with an ominous frontal breeze from the west. The sky turned gray. Lightning shot down from low clouds over Slim Buttes. All around us, and closing in. Flies huddled on the screen. From the leading edge of the storm, heavy droplets of rain began to fall.

They wouldn't make it before the storm hit.

Finally Ashley asked, "Do you think you could give us a ride home?"

The solenoid grudgingly started "Dorf," the gray, beat-up pickup truck.

"Go faster," the kids urged from the back as we approached the roller-coaster loop-de-loops in the S-curve approaching the cut-across, squealing with delight as the truck lifted off the springs.

Returning to their tiny, third-world 14 x 16-foot home, Josh and Eric got out down on the strip, heading up a narrow path without looking back. Ashley, the boys, and the dog got out at their trailer house. Couldn't see any adults around. Maybe. Maybe not.

Anywhere else in America—Boston, New York, Florida, California, and sure enough Colorado—they'd say those kids were "at risk." Everyone here knows that's true of the entire population.

Armageddon Didn't Happen Yet

Since Y2K came and went, and that fly-by asteroid sailed on by without hitting us and sending planet earth back into the Stone Age, and since that last solar mass ejection blew past us without shutting down all our satellites, and that planet on the other side of the sun hasn't caused a planetary polar shift, and California hasn't slid into the Pacific, and Florida isn't underwater, and all those planets lining up this past summer didn't make everything down here go out of kilter, we've been going ahead as usual.

"It doesn't change anything we're doing over here," said Joe American Horse.

Actually, Uncle Joe was referring to the stinging articles appearing in *Indian Country Today* (which actually had a decent run of commentaries on the subject presenting different views) and the *Lakota Journal* denouncing the practice of Lakota ceremonies (Sun Dance and sweat lodge) by non-Indians, but the quote still applies, even though the polar ice cap does appear to be turning to slush, and the current U.S. government has finally almost admitted the possibility of global warming.

"We're still going to do what we've got to do," said Uncle Joe.

And it's true. We're still plugging along here with local projects and ceremonies with our racially diverse groups of summer volunteers, Germans, and tourists passing through, leaving in their wake a new kitchen, finished greenhouse, clean garden, and impressive new timber-frame field office, still under construction.

Pine Ridge being the welfare state that it is, ALL resources, from people-power to government commodities, come from the outside. With over three-fourths of the population unemployed, one could guess that not much is being produced here.

Accordingly, whatever industry occurs here is a result of interested parties bringing to the reservation their energy, skills, and resources, combined with the drive of the locals to make it happen. In the case of this Slim Buttes neighborhood, it's mostly Tom Cook, the driving force behind the gardening program and attempts to introduce industrial hemp agriculture as a means for economic development and productive land use.

So, right now, he's down over the hill, working by light bulb on his impressive new field office with Sal Lame. The crew of eight guys he started with all took off after the first or second payday, except for Rusty, who stayed on the project to work with Steve. Steve Chappel, the man who wrote the book on traditional timber framing, left yesterday after going with Rusty to take in an all-night birthday ceremony in Pine Ridge. He looked thoroughly exhausted on his way out, headed to the airport.

Steve and his workshop teams built the two greenhouses in Slim Buttes last year, and just this past month they constructed the new field office that Tom is still working on down there under a lightbulb.

Just before Steve and his teams from Maine came here to do their thing, a carpentry crew from Plenty, a group from The Farm community in Summertown, Tennessee, came up to build a screened-in addition to the kitchen they built last fall. It was the same group that did the initial frame construction on the hemp house, which, incidentally, is still standing empty.

They're thinking about putting handicapped ramps on it so Ernest can get in and out. Ernest is now at Tom and Loretta's. He still can't walk and has no use of his right side yet, but he's talking now, eating, and has had the stomach tube removed. He's slowly coming around and wants to go back into sweat lodge as soon as possible. Still, he's confined to a wheelchair for now, until all your prayers come through.

So, despite what others may say about preserving The Ways just for Indians, it was Ernest, and before him, his brother, Larue, who simply said, "Anyone who wants to pray with us can come pray."

And so, why shouldn't we? What can indigenous people offer those who bring their energy, skills, and resources to the reservation? What can The People offer the world?

According to some, the pipe and the spiritual ways of The People are about all that is left that is worth anything, and they're all that is left. That's why some wish to see it preserved, protected, and unadulterated. But, like your last food in the house, it is put out for The People, saying, "This is all I've got to offer."

Milo Yellow Hair summed it up here recently, saying, "What you had here was a clash of cultures, where the natural inclination of one was to give and the other was to take. So it worked out fine. They got it all, and we ended up with nothing."

And so now, here in the twenty-first century, before the polar ice cap melts, we're hoping this may change.

Slim Buttes Horse
Latitudes

Some days we don't get much accomplished. That fly at the corner of my mouth got me up before sunrise, so I went ahead and made a pot of coffee, expecting Milo to stop by with that pack of smokes from town from the five bucks I gave him when he left here yesterday.

The ground was soupy yesterday from Saturday's rain, but passable back here on the grass. Too soupy for the annual Running Strong bus tour of mostly octogenarians to try to make it down over the hill to check out "the grounds" and projects they help fund.

I thought I could make it out in Dorf, so I loaded up the chain saw to cut wood, since it's already getting chilly at night, and . . . we always need wood. Dorf just growled. Wouldn't start. Not even close.

Grrrrrrrrrrrrrr. That solenoid that's been acting up for the past month finally gave out. It's a "no go."

Stranded. Dead in the water. Slim Buttes Horse Latitudes.

In exchange for taking the stitches out of his head from the stabbing, Sal removed the starter when he and Cetan came up from over the hill where they were working. In addition to the head wound, Sal had incurred another injury to his hand, slicing it open on a sheet of metal roofing they were trying to get installed before the tour came through. A tough couple of days for Sal.

Rumor was that the crew had been drinking, each of them pointing the finger at the other.

Milo, however, wasn't drinking when he received the hammer blow to the head up in Porcupine, I think it was. Maybe Wounded Knee. Twelve stitches to close it.

"The guy came up to my van and said, 'What the hell's going on?'" said Milo. "The next think I knew was . . . POW. I sort of saw it coming out of the corner of my eye, so I didn't take the full impact directly."

That was his good friend, he said, that he had known all his life. Assault with a deadly weapon.

With Sal, it was his old lady. Head wounds. A knife and a hammer. Alcohol-induced incidents.

"Yeah," I told Sal. "Hacuna matata. No problemo. I can take 'em out. Just sit here and lean your head back."

— — — — —

Been raining for two days straight, turning the local area to impassable gumbo. Gray, cold, wet, and drizzly. A good day for assisted suicide. Even if the truck was running, I wouldn't be able to get out of here. Not uncommonly, the Thunderbeings waited until the fourth door of ceremony Sunday night to come through and saturate the area.

A good day for salamanders and art projects. Began chiseling out drum frames from the logs Milo and I cut the other day, after being told by the kids who walked over here last week where there were some good hollow cottonwood logs down by the church, down by the river, they said.

— — — — —

In the middle of three projects. Got wood chips littering the kitchen from the three drum frames chiseled out and waiting for that buffalo hide to soak enough for the hair to "slip."

Ratchets and snap-on sockets scattered around after a greasy, contortionist attempt to replace the starter.

Up under the wheel well . . . over the steering suspension . . . under the frame . . . up between the manifold . . . "What moron engineer designed . . . ?"

As a writer with the hands of a typist, I HATE getting greasy or working on engines. It's not that I can't.

I'd just rather pay straight out, or maybe make a trade for auto mechanical work, like, "I'll remove your stitches if you remove my starter." That's a pretty good trade.

But since Sal didn't come back with Cetan and Mary when they slithered back here in the mud and brought the new starter in here this morning, I found myself up under that truck, with hopes of attending the powwow tonight. Maybe pick up a few groceries and a pack of smokes.

Got wet and filthy. Got the starter on, too. For that third, ill-conceived, awkward bolt up on top, you've got to have a six-inch extension, a half-inch-deep socket, and the flexibility of Stretch Armstrong. Otherwise, forget it.

"Okay, Baby. Let's seeeee." Started right up. Unfortunately, once it started, the starter wouldn't disengage.

"You'll have to bring it in," said Mike, down at Hill's Tire in Chadron, over the phone. "If you drive it like it is, you'll fuse the starter to the flywheel."

Great.

———

I guess it was the Spaniards who gave that space in the ocean its name. They'd sit for days, somewhere within thirty degrees north of the equator, waiting for a breeze, sending men out in boats to oar their galleons into a new current. To lighten their loads, they'd catapult overboard everything that wasn't absolutely necessary for the round-trip voyage to the New World, including the horses.

Queen Isabella's mission, and horses whose hooves would never touch the earth of the Americas. Lost in the Horse Latitudes. Dead in the water.

———

With fall approaching, the flies are on the screen in droves, endeavoring to effect entry into the house. I asked Milo, who was sitting here drinking coffee with Cetan, if he thought those flies, just prior to the moment of their death, had that premonition of something about to hit them, like he said he did when that guy struck him with the hammer.

"They must," he said. "They've got a thousand eyes."

Cetan laughed and said, "They tell each other, 'You watch my back, and I'll watch yours.'"

"Don't have to," laughed Milo, speaking for the fly. "Just watch your own ass. I've got mine covered."

In the manner of Lupe, and Scarface, we talk to the flies. "I tried to tell you, but you no listen." WHAP.

"NOW look at you."

There's another. "Wellll, Old Fly," reaching for the swatter. "You've done made me get up."

"You've made your last walk. YOU won't be waking me up tomorrow." There's one on the saucer.

WHAP. Dead in the water.

Disposable People

Ever try to fix your automatic coffeepot? It's not designed to be fixed. Those little hex screws on the bottom aren't supposed to be removed. If it's broken, you're supposed to throw it away and go get a new one.

Maybe a Mr. Coffee. Maybe a Bunn this time. Need the clock? The timer? Want auto shut-off? Wake-up feature? Top shelf, or low-end Wal-Mart special? Nine ninety-five gets you a pretty simple affair. A water reservoir, a heating element, and rubber hoses connecting the water intake and delivery lines to an upper dispenser. If anything goes wrong, it can't be much, you'd think.

As a culture, we don't fix much. Coffeepots, relationships, the reservation. We tend to move on.

Disposed memories. Discarded history. Discarded people.

When we heard that loud "Crack!" we first thought it was the carafe, but we later learned it was the hot water forcing one of the rubber water lines free from its coupling and the sound of the hot water spitting out all at once, onto the counter, onto the floor.

The coffeepot had been overworked and needed something comparable to angioplasty. It had, after many months of dependable service, become slow and feeble, incapable of meeting the demands of "the boys," who, nearly all, have returned.

People leave for a variety of reasons, but never because of a job. Usually it's a woman, alcohol, or pride.

Sometimes it's a combination. But then they come back.

Wes came back two weeks ago, sober, bright, working steady, and looking to return again to the circle of the sweat lodge. He said he hadn't been able to come around for the past six months because of the ankle bracelet.

"What does it take (to overcome alcohol), Wes?" we asked, wondering about some of the other members of "the crew."

"It took all that," he said, sitting at the table with a cup of coffee. "That," meaning arrest, threat of long-term incarceration, probation, treatment, and six months of ankle bracelet. "But really," he continued, "it's up to the person themselves, making up their mind to quit. I kept thinking about my kids."

Guys will leave, you won't see them for awhile, then they'll come back. Like Lupe, who came back today for the first time since last spring, after leaving a sad message on the answering machine last night saying he wanted to return to his spiritual traditions. "Back with the bros," he said.

Wes brought him out from Pine Ridge Village, hung over with the DTs, alcohol heavy on his pores, and a large, fresh gash right in the middle of his head from "a bottle," he said. Dead center. Looked like he'd been up all night. Pitiful, but sober, wanting coffee, wanting sugar.

"I feel like hell," he said.

Aloysius, who had come up from over the hill, teased him. "What'sa matter? You have no ears? I tried to tell you, but you no listen." Lupe, still hurting, just laughed.

Cetan and Mary Horse came by with another guy who sat outside in the car, then left. Tom dropped in, then went over the hill to harvest his garden. Aloysius wondered why the coffeepot was so slow. Lupe was on his feet, walking around the kitchen, unnecessarily apologetic. We encouraged him to join us later to sweat out the toxins.

"Tell her next time," we teased, "'Baby, could you hit me one more time? Except this time, maybe use a hammer?'"

Wes took off over the hill while Al, Lupe, and I stretched a large, blue square of plastic tarp over the netting over the deck that provided about two hours of shade until the wind picked up. Disassembled the coffeepot, gave it open-heart treatment, reconnected the hoses, and put it back together, twice, after the first attempt proved ineffective in its resuscitation.

Milo showed up in the early afternoon and started the fire, then Ron, then Owen, everyone wanting coffee.

Tom came back over the hill with Craig Lee from Kentucky, another guy who keeps coming back and is staying down over the hill in the camper with the intention of working on the hemp house up until the time of Alex White Plume's civil court date next month with the Drug Enforcement Agency for hemp cultivation.

Full moon with coyotes howling up close down on the river. Around the fire was news of the latest three-car auto fatalities just last night, and deaths from hair spray and rubbing alcohol, and tribal politics for what's going to make life better for The People, like that road out there that's so bad that when those people hit one of its holes, their car thought it had been in a wreck, activating the air bag that dislocated his jaw and fractured her neck.

Nine of us went into the lodge. No elders. Upon emerging two hours later, Lupe exclaimed, "That was a hot one!" to which Aloysius retorted as he toweled off on a nearby log, "You'd better get used to it. It's going to be a lot hotter where you're going."

We stood in the moonlight around the fire, staring until just glowing embers remained.

Afterward in the kitchen, the coffeepot was working but nobody wanted any coffee. Wes and Lupe took off for Pine Ridge, since Wes has work first thing in the morning. The remaining guys sat around the kitchen table eating orange slices and Oreos, with the talk eventually degenerating to the war in Afghanistan, depleted uranium laser-guided explosives, the 4.5 billion-year shelf-life of U238 isotopes, and the rendering of Mother Earth as a radiation cesspool.

And then we had a lively discussion about building a championship circuit skateboard park up at Oglala.

An Indian
Thanksgiving

Last week, in between rounds during the sweat lodge, Aloysius announced that he'd like to have a surprise birthday/thanksgiving peyote meeting in honor of his sister, Loretta. He wanted to have it in the "Old Place," the run-down church house just over the hill.

"Nothing big," he said, first in Lakota, addressing Ernest, who was conducting the lodge, then repeated his announcement in English. "Just a small one. Just family," he said.

"Just a small one," Tom said later, laughing. "About two hundred dollars worth."

We laughed, because it takes about five hundred bucks to throw, or sponsor, a peyote meeting. You gotta have the "medicine," you've got to ask a "Peyote Road Man," or minister in the Native American Church, to come conduct the ceremony, and you gotta toss a couple hundred dollars his way to cover the travel expenses for him and his family.

You've gotta prepare all the food for breakfast and the main meal and have the sacred food ready. You've got to put up a tipi. You've got to get a lot of wood together, enough to last all night. There's a lot of things you've got to have lined out. You've got to have a "cedar man" and a fireman. You've got to have helper cooks. Gotta have a lot of gophers. What that meant for Tom is that he's going to be doing a lot of the work.

Between that announcement and the actual event yesterday, the cat got out of the bag and Loretta ended up finding out about it from her husband Tom's big mouth, according to Aloysious, so there went the surprise.

"She's GOTTA know," said Tom, in self-defense. "She's got the MONEY."

Well, that's okay, because very little happens around here without Tom and Loretta being involved, primarily by virtue of them having most of the resources.

Then Beatrice, naturally, had to be involved. The mother of Aloysious and Loretta, and matriarch in the lineage of a medicine family, she's the one who had to "line it all out," although many people would probably like to take credit for it. Fact is, many people come together to pull it off. But officially, Beatrice and Aloysious were the sponsors.

The "medicine," the peyotes, turned out to be really strong and clean, according to those who "took in," or participated. Beatrice had prepared the three sacred wasnas (sacred food) that are used: the corn, the chokecherry, and the dried buffalo meat.

Turned out, in addition to celebrating Loretta's birthday, they were going to include a formal "hunka," a making of relatives ceremony and naming ceremony, including Loretta's brother Poncho, her sister Nita, and Poncho's son Norman, who had just had his eighth birthday.

Kurt Fool Bull, Willard's brother, whom they invited over from Rosebud Reservation to run the ceremony, took Norman as a nephew; Charlotte Black Elk took Nita as a sister; Sharon Fool Bull, wife of Willard, took Poncho as a brother; and Loretta's uncle, Richard Broken Nose, gave her the name 'Anpetu Luta Winyan.' Beatrice was doing this for her three children and her grandson.

During the ceremony, each of these new relations stands behind the person they are taking as a relative, ties an eagle plume or feather in their hair, and loudly announces four times to those assembled the new Indian name given to each of the recipients who are being honored.

Prayers, short speeches, and songs accompany the ceremony. The people circle outside the tipi, stopping in the Four Directions, following the singer, and re-enter. A pipe is loaded and smoked, and at the end, the honorees give away some nice gifts to their new relative. Shawls, star quilts, blankets, beaded moccasins, cushions, chairs, and the very tipi was given away.

I got invited three times to attend the meeting, along with my kids who were here for the holiday, so we went up the next day for the hunka and main meal after Tom came over here looking for a drum, but we didn't "take in" the night before. I sent over a half truckload of wood, and we just listened from over here.

"You guys gotta come over and eat with us," he said. "There's a ton of food."

Everyone's faces were glowing red from sitting up all night with the medicine, all "peyotied up," as they say. All those folks I just named were there, along with Uncle Ernest, Uncle Joe American Horse, the families of Kurt and Sharon from Rosebud; Raymondo Eagle Bear, who served as fireman throughout the night, and Nita's boyfriend, Earl.

For the benefit of Digger and Mia, Uncle Joe, wearing his headdress and full regalia, spoke in English. He explained the ceremony and the important personages who were there, each representing a long line of medicine families and people who have kept the ancient traditional ceremonies alive to this day, naming off the seven sacred rites of the Oglala, including this hunka and naming ceremony.

After the ceremony, we all went inside the Old Place for the birthday and thanksgiving dinner. Inside the poor, dilapidated "church house" that sits humbly out in the middle of heaven were three tables piled high with food. There were five different flat cakes. Enough pumpkin, apple, and peach pies for everyone there to take a whole one home; three huge vats of artery-blocking soup that everybody loves; had to be four or five turkeys; a huge box of fry bread; candy salad; two huge pans of stuffing; mashed potatoes and gravy; cranberries; tuna salad; juice and coffee; ice cream; a big container of cookies; dried buffalo meat; a huge tub of expanding dough that was never needed for more fry bread; and one hundred-proof, cold peyote tea sitting on the stove for whomever besides Digger might want it. From the looks of it, it looked like overkill.

They sang birthday songs, opened and read the cards aloud, gave away some presents and cash, and proceeded to eat. After eating, everybody loaded up their "watecha" buckets to take all the rest of the food home to their relatives. Nothing was expected to be left. That food would be spread far and wide, feeding many people beyond the actual meeting for several days.

As people finished eating, Kurt explained that we wouldn't just toss out that sacred "morning water" that comes into the tipi in the morning after fasting with the medicine throughout the night. The "first medicine," as they say, and Kurt said there was some left in the bucket, and he'd take it around, sun-wise, and we'd all finish it off.

"There's been good prayers made over this water," he said.

Everybody said, "Aho," in affirmation, and he took it around, each person drinking from the small cup, taking care not to spill a drop.

Too Extreme

"Rumor has it there's a chicken in here," said Milo, dipping a spoon into the pot of chicken and noodle soup on the stove. He turned to the crowd in the kitchen and laughed his low, coarse, unique, and contagious laugh. Seems there's never enough meat in the soup.

The guys chuckled in response as they huddled around the kitchen table, focused, heads lowered over coffee cups of hot soup. We had just come from the sweat lodge. Five degrees outside. One degree for each of the five of us that went in. Didn't hang around the fire afterward. Everyone raced first to their cars, then right up to the house.

"MAN, that was severe!" said Tom, stomping his feet inside the door and heading straight to the wood stove. The other fellas followed, tracking mud across the kitchen floor. People warmed up, then headed for the soup and coffeepot. Tom grabbed the mop, and we joked about who had the most experience with a mop.

"I go waaaaaay back with a mop," he said, as he swabbed the floor.

"There ain't nuthin' 'bout a mop that I don't know."

The guys laughed and ate and decompressed from the lodge.

Aloysious had arrived after the second round and respectfully "watched the door" ("doorman" for the lodge), and Owen was there earlier, but he left at sundown, just as we were putting the fire together. It was freezing, with the wind blowing from the north. "The wind blew the lodge apart," said Milo. It would be a hassle and a challenge to put the tarps back on in the wind.

"Uh huh," said Owen. Then he got in his car and left and never came back.

"Too severe," Al said later at the kitchen table. "Besides that, I don't like to walk into ceremony once it's already started . . . you know, Bro, out of respect. That's the way I was taught . . . and it's too damn cold coming out."

True. True. Yet, there's something entirely strengthening and invigorating when sweating in such conditions, as you may know—of stepping from a steaming sweat lodge into the snow. They say some people wallow in the snow or take a dip in a river. We don't do that.

We towel off and head right for the soup pot.

Milo and I stacked and lit the fire, then put the lodge back together just at dark. Two hours later, the stones were ready. Tom and Ron showed up. Then Ben Good Buffalo.

"No kids, no girls. You can turn it up on high, Bro," I told Tom, making a dial-turning motion with my hand as we shed our clothes at the fire before light-footing it across frozen ground to the lodge doorway.

Just Tom, Ben, Milo, Ron (who'd just returned from L.A.), and me.

Tom turned it up on high. After the second round, Ron, panting and down on his elbows, said, "You guys are extremists!"

Yeah. Sort of. As a way of life, the Sun Dance road, relative to other ways, could be viewed as extreme, especially when viewed from the seat of a tour bus, looking down on the fourth day in the arbor. The people aboard the bus might think those people out there in the sun are extremists. (We dance on private grounds, the Wild Horse Sanctuary in the Black Hills at the invitation of the owner, Mr. Dayton Hyde, who also operates tours of the grounds that includes petroglyphs, a movie set, and us, the four summer solstice days we're there. The bus stops a respectful distance away, high on a hill, and prohibits photographs. No doubt a pagan ritual in their eyes; we see it more as an offering.)

So yeah, relatively speaking, compared to other paths where much isn't asked of a person other than to try to be a good person, one could say what we do is extreme. It doesn't make us any more enlightened; in fact, sometimes we get stupider (as twelve-year-old Kandice says, "Boys go to Jupiter to get stupider . . . girls go to Mars to get candy bars," and around here, it sure enough looks like that's a fact), but one could also say we're trying to maintain an open link or perhaps simply do what the old men told us to do: "Keep it going."

"I'm depending on you guys to keep this going," Ernest said one night after his incapacitation.

"In honor of our ancestors, and as a mandate from our elders, it is what we must do. If we don't, it dies out."

That's what Tom said several years ago when I asked him why he put so much effort into the Dance and the Native American Church and the twice-weekly lodge. A truckload of wood, a load of tipi poles, twenty bucks for the elder who needed gas to get there . . .

It is our time. It is upon us. We've got elders looking back and young people looking forward. That's why it's so encouraging when both are present at ceremonies. The elders for their leadership, and the young folks to learn and carry on. The generations up and down the line, right there, alive and real in the here and now 3-D world.

And when it's gray and freezing outside, the truck is snow-covered and looking like it might not feel like starting, the dogs are wincing in the wind, and the birds are fluffed up, scratching for seed, and it looks like a lot of work out there around the lodge, those are the times you might think you're not up for it, thinking folks might call and say, "Let's cancel it."

But by midday, when the sun pops through a hole in the clouds, the phone starts ringing from expectant people, and Milo pulls up with a load of fresh stones . . . what did the Old Men say do?

Put on the long johns. Put on a pot of coffee.

Epilogue

Two years have passed since the writing of the last essay. We just completed our seventh year Sun Dancing in the canyon, and are preparing right now for the eighth. There are success stories, men overcoming alcohol and overwhelming odds to stand strong as warriors among their families and The People. They are our heroes.

People continue to die. Bernard Red Cloud Sr. and Uncle Solomon Red Bear died, along with some little ones in tragic accidents. More teens have died in auto wrecks. More kids are at risk.

When America is having a hard time, life then becomes especially difficult for many of her native people—still forgotten, marginalized, or ignored altogether. Over here, everywhere I look, I see The People struggling.

We rely on one another, get by and keep the fire lit.

About the Author

Vic Glover is a Vietnam vet combat medic, a former journalist, and professor of communication. He writes humor, political satire, and social commentary from his home on Pine Ridge Reservation.

Native Voices

 tribal legends, medicine, arts & crafts,
history, life experiences, spirituality

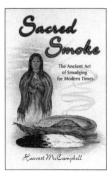

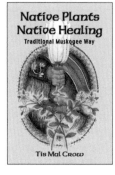

Sacred Smoke
The Ancient Art of
Smudging for Modern
Times
Harvest McCampbell
1-57067-117-6 $9.95

Native Plants
Native Healing
Traditional Muskogee
Way
Tis Mal Crow
1-57067-105-2 $12.95

Plants of Power
Native American
Ceremony and the Use of
Sacred Plants
Alfred Savinelli
1-57067-130-3 $9.95

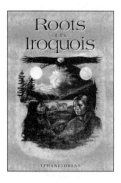

Sisters in Spirit
Iroquois Influence on Early
American Feminists
Sally Roesch Wagner
1-57067-121-4 $14.95

Roots of the Iroquois
Tehanetorens
1-57067-097-8 $9.95

Purchase these Native American titles from your local bookstore
or you can buy them directly from:

Book Publishing Company • P.O. Box 99 • Summertown, TN 38483
1-800-695-2241

Please include $3.95 per book for shipping and handling.